The Dread Champion

Jacob Peterson

ISBN: 978-0-578-29520-6

Edited by Edie Mourey (www.furrowpress.com).
Book production by Scribe Books, Nashville, TN.
Cover artwork by Cody Pratt.
Book design by Brianna Showalter, Ruston, WA.

Dedication

To my wife, Lexie Peterson.

You showed me the love of Jesus in my darkest hour.
When you had every right to cast stones,
you said with the same words of our Savior,
"Neither do I condemn you, go and sin no more."

Thank you for standing with me and fighting for me.

I love you,
Jacob

Acknowledgements

Lexiegirl: Thank you for your love and constant voice of encouragement in my life. You are an incredible wife, mother, and disciple of Jesus Christ. You are my best friend and my daily promise that God is faithful to His Word. I love you! *

Rhys, Piper, and Olive: I love you all so much. Being your Father is the greatest joy of my life, you all have taught me so much about the love of the Father. You will always be my little girls.

Mom: Thank you for fighting on my behalf through intercession, I truly believe I am where I am today because of your prayers. Little did you know your prayers were on behalf of a generation that would one day read this book, thank you for your YES!

Dad: Thank you for always being there for me. Some of the greatest life lessons I have learned have come from watching you. You taught me how to catch fish and to be a Husband and Father that loves his family. Thank you.

Heath and Macey: I love you both so much. I am so thankful to call you my brother and sister. Your faith and devotion to Jesus constantly challenges me to love Jesus more. Heath, your friendship has helped me through some of my darkest times. From playing N64 as kids to standing beside each other on our wedding days. You'll always be my big brother who I look up to!

Aunt Wanda, Uncle Rob, April, Frankie, Harley and Ryder: I am so grateful for you all. Your love for me and my family brings so much joy to my life. Thank you for always being there for us.

To all of Lexie's siblings and their spouses: One of the best parts of marrying Lexie was becoming a part of your family. I love you all so much.

Karen Wheaton: Thank you for being the real deal and teaching me how to, "Love Him and Love them." Your passion for Jesus has ruined me for normal.

Aaron Burke: Your voice in my life has been instrumental in seeing this giant of pornography fall. I am so grateful for you and Katie and the example you have set forth.

Dr. Evon Horton: Thank you for taking a chance on a young minister who was just starting out. I learned life lessons at Brownsville that I still carry with me today.

Bobby Sasser: So thankful for our friendship that started as interns at Brownsville. From launching churches to doing kettlebell squats in your driveway, I am looking forward to a lifetime of friendship.

Cody Nelms: Since the days of the print shop you have been a source of joy in my life, I am so thankful to call you brother and friend.

Ramp Leadership: The OG Chosen!! You have been my heroes ever since I first saw you all going after Jesus in black and camo. Thank you for being the role models I needed to run this race strong.

Dr. Doug and Paula Ley: Thank you for teaching me the radical middle and for pouring so much into my family and me. The Lamb is worthy!

Edie Mourey: You helped me listen to the voice of the Lord in writing this book and helped me tap into His heart for this project. Thank you!

Dan Depriest: It was such a pleasure to work with you, thank you for your valuable wisdom and insight into this project.

Foreword

Everyone wants to get free, but very few know how to live free. For the past 2 decades, I have delt with male after male who has come to me bound by pornography. They have tried, prayed, fasted and yet the vicious cycle continued. What is the solution?

At the risk of sounding old, I think sexual temptation is worse for this upcoming generation than ever before. Pornographic material is more prevalent and more accessible than any time in the history of mankind. 100 years ago, for a person to see someone naked, they literally had to hire a prostitute or to physically go to a strip club. Today, that same person only has to install an app on their phone. What was a risky public sin has now become a rampant private addiction.

The impact of the sexualization of our culture is overwhelming. Pornography is killing people's joy, their marriage, their ministry, and most importantly their intimacy with God. It is rare to find a man or woman who has found total freedom in this area of their life.

What our culture needs is fresh purity revolution. Purity has unfortunately become a dirty word because of the misuse and manipulation of some church leaders in the decades past. This must change. We need purity to be popular again. What do we do? This is where the book in your hand is going to help.

I have known Jacob since he was a wild, passionate teenager. He moved to Pensacola and interned at the youth ministry that I had the honor of leading. Jacob stood out from the rest because of his intense passion for God and the purity of his heart. He lives with an aim of genuinely pleasing God.

Jacob is also one of the best preachers I have met. He can deliver dynamic truths from God's word in a compelling way. He has the perfect mixture of humor and depth. From a distance, Jacob is the perfect Christian guy.

No one wants to learn from the Christian that has it all together. For years I have told upcoming leaders that people are impressed by your strengths, but they are impacted by your weaknesses. In this book, Jacob opens up with extreme vulnerability his battle with pornography.

This book was not a shock to me. I have been part of Jacob's story for a long time and it is was his honestly about his struggle that gave me so much hope for his freedom. Everyone has issues. You have issues. If you don't think you have issues, well that is your issue. The question is not "do you have issues?" The question is "are you able to be honest about your issue?"

We are all as healthy as we are honest. In the same way, we are all as sick as our secrets. If you are struggling, there is hope for you. You are about to dive into a book that is uniquely written. It is both engaging and challenging. You will receive hope. Let Jacob's testimony be the catalyst for the freedom you can receive in Christ. You might have stumbled, but your story is not over. Get back up. Try again. We need a healthy version of you. A free you. Let the journey begin.

Aaron Burke
Lead Pastor, Radiant Church

—

Incredible preacher, pastor, and leader, Jacob Peterson reveals how to find freedom from pornography and sexual sin through his own story of deliverance.

The Dread Champion offers readers an incredible journey through the allegory of Clay and his pilgrimage to find freedom and identity. There are so many people trapped in the darkness of sexual perversion and bound to the addiction of pornography with no hope for freedom. But, through Jacob's personal story, readers can discover the deliverance and redemption found only in Jesus Christ.

For people seeking identity and a generation in desperate need of truth, this book is a guide into to the presence of God to discover that reality. This inspirational content gives you biblical insight into how the enemy works in his attempts to keep you bound in sexual sin. Enjoy the story of Clay and learn how God wants to bring you into deliverance and set you in a place of prosperity. Be equipped with the tools to overcome sexual sin and live a life filled with the purpose of God for your life.

Don't get stuck in your past failures or sins or allow present circumstances to keep you from living in true freedom. Let Dread Champion be a resource to lead you into the fullness of the plan God has for your life.

Karen Wheaton
Founder and Senior Leader of The Ramp

CONTENTS

CHAPTER 1

THE DISCOVERY

I do it. I look. I stare. I fall to pornography again.

I thought I was done with it—forever done—but I was wrong. It has been years since I saw my first pornographic image, and time after time after thinking I've beaten this thing, it comes out of nowhere and levels me.

Sitting on the edge of my bed in silence, still in shock at what just happened, at what I did, I feel as though a 275-pound linebacker has slammed me to the ground. My chest is so compressed under the weight of guilt and shame that it's hard for me to take in a full breath.

I guess I shouldn't be surprised, but I am for some reason. I guess I wanted my last time to have been my last time.

Trying to right my wrong and convince myself as I delete the history off my phone, I say, barely audible, "This time it will be different. Now, *this* will be my *last* time!" If only I could believe myself.

Being two different people is difficult to do; it's a weighty burden to bear. The person who is addicted to porn is not the person everyone knows and loves. In public, I wear a smile everywhere I go, projecting strength and confidence. The person I am behind closed doors, however, no one knows except for me and God, of course.

Finally, I stand up, knowing I have to go out and face the world with a smile even though I feel like a failure—no, even though I *am* a failure. But once I'm on my feet, I don't move. I can't summon the power to leave my room as if nothing has happened. I don't have the gumption to pretend anymore.

The flicker of hope in my heart starts to dwindle more and more with every breach of the promises I've made to myself of no more porn. What was once a vibrant flame inside that caused me to believe I could overcome my hidden addiction has turned into a pile of embers with little to no hope of rekindling.

"God, I have no excuse, no justification for my action, but I've got to get this burden off my chest. I've asked for forgiveness and freedom from this more times than I can remember. I don't even know if it's worth asking again. But I need You to touch me. I need You to change me! I'm desperate!"

Silence. That's all I get. Loud, deafening silence.

The truth is God could be talking to me right now. He could be saying something, but I know my guilt and shame are in the way. They're like noise-canceling headphones that void out the sound of His voice.

I still can't leave my room. I can't put on the fake smile. I can't face another familiar face of someone who would be disappointed or disgusted by my succumbing to my addiction yet again. I can't keep up the lies. I need—I have to get away!

I will retreat into the woods rather than show my face to anyone right now. I figure I can get away from the Internet, technology, and people. Like Jacob in the Bible, when he sent his family and friends away, I need to be alone; I need to wrestle with God. He has to touch me as He did Jacob—so that my walk looks different and I get a new name.

Determined not to come back out of those woods the same, I walk out of my bedroom and into the hallway leading to the back door of my house. I need to find my gear if I'm going to stay in the woods for a few days.

The screen door slams shut behind me as I make my way toward the shed.

I've always loved the outdoors and camping. My dad took my brother and me when we were young, and he made it a great time. It's been a while since I've gone myself, though.

Entering into the shed, I scan the piles of stuff shoved in the corners. My eyes catch a glimpse of some boxes I remember cramming my camping gear into. "They would have to be on the bottom of a huge leaning pile of cardboard boxes," I grunt as I make my way around stuff that I should have hauled out of there a long time ago, kicking some of it out of my path.

I stand before the pile and begin hefting off each box. Finally, I get to my camping gear where I find my hatchet, tent, lantern, headlamp, and old pair of hiking boots. So glad the boots still fit because all I've been wearing boot-wise these days are Chelsea boots. I'm more than happy to trade in my trendy pull-ons for my old ones that I have to lace up.

"There's my backpack pushed up against the wall beside the bottom box. Perfect! I can throw all this stuff in it. All I need now is food, water purifier, and some clothes—then I'll be set!" I say aloud to nobody present. The backpack is a Kelty internal frame with all kinds of cool features built to carry whatever I need. Nice how something with gadgets can get my mind off myself.

I go back to the house to get the rest of my stuff for a weekend away. Of course, I purposely leave Enemy Number One behind; that's my laptop. But I grab food supplies, my clothes, my Bible, a pen, and my journal, quickly cramming everything into my sturdy pack, and then I storm the front door like a soldier off to battle.

Throwing my pack into the back of my Jeep, I hop in behind the wheel and spin out of my driveway. Still weighed down by my failure, I drive down the road in silence. No music blasting. I'm not in the mood. No sound but the wind whipping around me. I think it's helping to clear my head.

After about an hour's drive, I arrive at a heavily forested area with a clearing where I can park my Jeep. It's at the beginning of the trail. It's a lonesome spot, very secluded. I take time to text a couple of family members with my location so they know where I am. I tell them I'm going off the grid, offering them no reason for the trek. I wait a few minutes until I receive their texts acknowledging mine. Then, I turn off my phone.

It's just me and God now. A guaranteed recipe for change— or trouble.

I'm familiar with this trail, so I begin to make my way to a special spot I found several years ago. I walk and look around, hearing Nature's sounds. It's on this trail that I begin to breathe more easily. I prefer the weight being on my back rather than sitting on my chest.

Hidden and far removed from temptation, I settle into my hike. I check my watch to clock my time and figure the distance into the woods. I realize I'm now beyond the reach of a cell tower, which means my phone can't connect me to any porn sites.

I continue hiking for about a few hours, stopping occasionally to rest and hydrate. I pass some decent places to set up camp, but I decide to keep going a little farther toward the special spot that's calling me. It's at the bluffs nearby, at least I think they're nearby. I have only been to the bluffs a couple times before. I discovered them by accident several years ago when I had followed the main trail back twelve to fifteen miles.

Back then, I was camping with my Dad and my brother, and I was just a kid. We were all walking together until I slowed down a little, a result of my growing tired from the long hike. My Dad and brother seemed to keep up their pace only a few yards ahead of me. But then I became separated from them after a bit because, while I was lagging behind them on the trail, I thought I saw something move back in the woods off the trail. I remember it stopped me cold, so I stood there terrified, scanning the woods for whatever was moving among the shadows of the trees.

Next thing I knew, Dad and my brother had continued without me, not realizing I had stopped, and they were then nowhere in view.

A little way ahead of me was a fork in the path. Left with only two options, of course I took the wrong one and lost my way. I remember being terrified. I began to run around looking desperately for something that looked familiar. That's when I found the bluffs. I was able to get to the top and scream as loudly as I could until they found me. I'll never forget the feeling when I heard my father's voice respond to my cries for help. Heading there now takes me back to that feeling of going from being lost to being found.

Much older today and on the trail alone, I keep moving for about an hour more until I find a sweet location. Even though the bluffs are yet out of view, I decide this is the perfect place to set up camp. It's nestled securely under a pair of towering pines. I like camping under pines because of the smell, and the needles create a pretty nice mattress under a sleeping bag. I set my pack down and pull out my tent. It has that musty storage smell, but everything is there and in good shape. I begin to go through the checklist in my mind, the checklist Dad taught me.

Tent. Check. Firewood. Check. Fire. Check.

I get so focused on building a fire that I fail to see the sun is hidden behind thick, dark storm clouds. The distant boom of thunder snaps me out of the zone. That's when I realize I had failed to check the weather before I left home.

I should be okay, I think. *After all, I came here to seek God, so if I am in my tent the whole time, I'll be fine. I only need a little time to get to the bluffs, and then I can come hang out here.*

Immediately, I grab my pack and set off toward the bluffs. Typically, I would mark my path, but if I remember correctly, I won't have to turn off the path I'm on to get to the bluffs. My dad would be so proud that I remembered the importance of marking a new trail. Being on a well-worn path, though, marking is unnecessary.

I look at my watch to check how long I've been walking when I hear some thunder. It sounds like it's far away. I decide to pull out my rain jacket from my pack and put it on, just in case. Placing my Kelty back over my shoulders, I begin walking again.

Several minutes elapse as I continue my walk. The wind picks up, and ominous clouds start to blanket the sky. *Sure glad I put on my rain jacket.* The thunder that was far off in the distance comes closer to me, and the trees begin to sway violently. *Swish-swoosh-whoosh.* The clouds unleash a downpour with lightning strikes cracking the earth. I pull my hood over my head.

Not wanting to risk getting caught on the bluffs in this storm, I turn around and begin to walk briskly back to camp. Soon, my eyes are unable to focus on the path as the rain is smacking me in the face, causing me to wince and blink rapidly. I tie my hood tighter around my face in order to keep my head dry, but it's definitely not protecting my face. Putting my left arm slightly above my forehead and holding tight to the strap of my backpack with my right hand, I try to continue back toward my dry tent.

Whack! My foot strikes something, tripping me. I fall forward, my knees hitting the ground first, but the weight of my upper body and my backpack cause me to tumble over and roll. A tree trunk catches my hip, stopping me. Completely prostrate on the muddy ground, I use the tree to help me stand up. Luckily, nothing's broken, but I'm not quite sure where I am—whether I'm even still on the trail.

"Don't panic. You'll be okay. You're not lost. You'll get back to camp," I try to steady myself.

I look over my right shoulder to get my bearings, because I can see better looking behind me as the rain isn't able to strike my face. I don't recognize anything to the right of me. So, I look over my other shoulder and see the bluffs. "They weren't there before," I mutter under my breath. I turn my head to the left again and see a dark hole among the bluffs.

"There's a cave! I can get out of this storm in there!"

Turning around, I run toward the cave, tripping over the uneven ground as I go. I don't remember seeing a cave at the bluffs before, but once I arrive at its entrance I am grateful I have a place to take refuge.

I drop my pack on the ground, right at the opening, and I dig through it, finding my headlamp. I pull it out and put it on. Flashing its light down the cavernous walls I look to see if anyone or anything else has decided to take refuge, too. I turn my head, moving the light from one side of the cave to the other, and then I yell out, "Hello! Is anyone in here?!"

My voice echoes back into the cave.

No one responds. I hear nothing after the echo stops.

It's a rather large cave that seems to wind pretty far back. I begin to walk around. I notice wood kind of tossed over against the wall of the cave opposite me. I figure it's probably left over from a previous tenant. I turn off my headlamp, and relying on the light at the opening of the cave, I pile up the wood, choosing some of the driest logs, and then take those to build a fire. Thankfully, the wood starts to burn well, helping me to warm up. Meanwhile, the rain shows no sign of stopping.

"Glad that's done. This will dry me out and warm me up real good and keep anything big and scary from coming in after me."

I begin to walk deeper into the cave—back as far as the light of the fire reaches—and then switch on my headlamp again to continue my search. As I walk, I get a little freaked out when I realize just how far back this thing goes. Funny how the mind can wander off in a dark cave. I start thinking of bears or escaped convicts living in here. Caves are creepy no matter what the circumstance is. The sounds of dripping water, the damp smell, and those nocturnal giant grasshopper things always make me uneasy.

I finally come to a stopping point, where the only way to go any farther is to kind of climb up some rocks that lead into a hole or tunnel of some sort about nine or ten feet above. I'm not too fond of the idea of getting trapped in a confined place by myself, but I can't help but be curious as to what I would find up in that hole. Instinctively, I strain to see what's in the hole above me if anything, and my headlamp light reveals the shadow of something hanging over the edge of what appears to be a ledge above.

Maybe it's an old knife or an animal bone. This area was pretty popular during the Gold Rush, so maybe it's the handle of a pickaxe or shovel. The cave begins to stir up my imagination.

Still not wanting to climb up and crawl through the narrow stricture, my inquisitive nature gets the best of me as I begin to look around to see how I could possibly get hold of whatever is up there. I find some outcroppings on the cave wall where I can get a good grip for my hands and feet to pull myself forward and kind of up. Once I have a solid base, I decide to push from my feet to sort of lunge up to reach my hand to the top of the ledge.

Whew! There, I've got the ledge. The fingers of my right hand dig into the rocky edge when, suddenly, my feet begin to slip. Knowing I'm about to fall, I push off the crumbling wall outcropping once more and grab ahold of whatever was sticking out from the ledge. It felt like leather.

"Got it!" I yell as I fall flat on my back with a loud *thud*! I land so hard that it knocks my lamp off my head. And whatever it is I grabbed on the way down is flung from my hand as my elbow slams against the cave floor.

"Great! About kill myself in this cave. That would be perfect— just perfect!"

I get up and try to slap off the sludge I assume is now on my backside.

"Now, where is that lamp?"

I find it a few feet away because, luckily for me, it's still shining. I put the head lamp back on my head and take in a couple of deep breaths. Apparently, that fall really knocked the wind out of me because it seems my lungs need more oxygen than what I can take in in a breath. My elbow is throbbing. I can move it, so it seems okay. Not broken, anyway. My backside is a little sore as well. Already tender from my tumble out in the rain, I figure I deserve to be a little sore back there given my last twenty-four hours.

Moving my head around to put light on the cave floor, I look for the object I pulled off the ledge. I notice something on the ground not too far from where I had fallen.

"That must be it!" I shout like a man who found treasure.

To my surprise, it's an old leather satchel. The leather is stiff and moldy but still in decent shape. I throw the bag over my shoulder and walk back to my fire at the mouth of the cave.

I reach the pile of wood, pick out some choice pieces, and throw them on the fire. The fresh timber causes the flames to spit and hiss. I gingerly sit down and try to get comfortable though my body now feels a bit achy. I begin to explore the contents of the satchel.

"Well, look here. There's an old pen, an old pocket watch, and a stag-handled knife. Isn't that something?! I thought I'd find a knife. Pretty cool! But what's this?"

Reaching deeper into the bag, I feel something else. Pulling it out, I see something wrapped in what seems to be a soft leather pelt. It looks like a journal.

The binding of the old journal cracks a little as I open it. The cover is brown leather that's a bit weathered by time and exposure. I'm amazed that the pages are still in great shape, however. The leather pelt must have protected them from the elements.

The fire continues to kindle inside while the rain pours outside as I open the journal and begin to read its contents. The text on the pages is handsomely artistic, handwritten in a masterful cursive by what must have required great care

This is what it says: "I want to tell you a story. It's my story. It may be your story. In the end, it's definitely His story."

CHAPTER 2

THE STORY

The opening lines of the journal are like words of a kind stranger inviting me to sit fireside and hear his tale or, should I say, our tale. I'm still a bit sore, so without hesitation, I place my pack behind my back and lean into it against the rocky wall, settling in for what seems to promise a welcome diversion from the storm that's still blowing outside and the darkness clouding my inner soul. And so, I begin to read . . .

In the mid-1800s, when the West was being pioneered and Native Americans still rode bareback across the Plains, there was a young man who had a heart for adventure. His name was Clay.

Clay was an ordinary young man. He came from a respected family who led a simple life. They stayed together, never caused trouble, and never went looking for adventure. They worked their land, paid their dues, and lived life by the Book.

Clay wasn't a rebel or an outcast, but he didn't fit his family mold. He wasn't satisfied with just living. He wanted more. He had dreams. He dreamt of the unknown, venturing out beyond safety, finding his own path in the world. He was led by his heart. His heart told him there was more: more than living sunrise to sunset, more than basic comforts, more than doing the same thing over and over again each and every day.

Clay wanted to be a man of more. He wanted to build something he could call his own. He wanted a life of risk, thrill, and riches. This dream of more was what caused him to leave his family, home, and everything he knew.

Clay soon told everyone he was leaving for guaranteed opportunity, but it was really for the thrill of adventure. Tales of war, survival, and dangerous beasts had been inviting him on a journey since he was a boy. When he was young, he remembered lying on the floor in front of the fireplace and listening to his grandfather tell stories of what it was like out West. His grandfather worked as a cattle hand for a while when he was younger and went on many trips out West driving cattle. One of Clay's favorite stories was when a "Blackfeet" raiding party came and tried to rob Grandfather and his compadres in the middle of the night.

It seems Grandfather was making his way back East with a group of French fur traders after he had finished his job driving cattle. These fur traders were of the roughest sort of men who lived in America those days. They would be in the wilderness for months on end without seeing another human being. They were experts in survival and combat.

One night, according to his grandfather, they sat around sharing stories in French and broken English. Out of nowhere, the calm, cool night was pierced by a war cry. Men began to scramble for their guns as arrows came from the darkness and into the light of the campfire. They started to fire into the direction of the arrows as Native American warriors came running toward them.

To the Native American, a war was not a necessary evil; it was the pathway to honor and manhood.

Clay's grandfather would tell Clay that he was able to fire off a couple of rounds in the night before he caught an arrow in the shoulder. Grandfather's adrenaline was rushing so strongly through his veins that he broke the arrow off and kept fighting. That night Grandfather jumped on his horse and rode off in the awful darkness, bleeding and afraid.

At some point in the story, Clay's grandfather pulled up his shirt and showed him the nasty scar the arrowhead had left over the blade of his shoulder. Wide-eyed and captivated, Clay was hooked. From that day forward, he daydreamed of going out West, the battles he would face, and the scars he would receive. It was no wonder that Clay was very excited when the time had finally come for him to journey westward.

Now, he was taking that journey with Virtue his horse. He and Virtue would find treasure and weather perilous storms, and he would win the fair maiden.

Clay's dreams were pushing, even pulling him into the unknown. He had no idea what was before him, but he knew he couldn't stay at home. He had to follow that deep, internal whisper that kept him awake at night and beckoned him to come and find the more.

———

This is incredible! I can't believe I get stuck in this cave and then happen upon a journal with a story that's actually interesting. Clay sounds like my kind of guy. He wants more, and more is calling him. Boy, can I relate.

I continue reading.

———

After months of travel, Clay found himself worn down and disappointed. He had expected to find adventure in the journey but instead encountered the loneliness of solitude and the constant discomfort that comes with riding on horseback and enduring hunger. Occasionally, he would make camp with fellow travelers. It was in these circles that he heard about Mount Yah.

As Clay sat around campfires with other travelers, the men would begin to speak of this infamous mountain. They described the perilous journey they or others they knew took to ascend Mount Yah, the hidden snares covered in its mystery, and its treasure beyond belief. The unknown, the mystery, and the promise of more drove Clay on. He knew he could conquer Mount Yah and claim the treasure for himself.

It wasn't too long before the mountain started to call to Clay in the night. He had dreams painted partly by the fireside tales he heard, but then there were other things in the dreams that were different. Sure, there was gold in the dreams—Clay's getting the gold, that is. He just knew the treasure was there for him for the taking. And he always dreamt about the rugged terrain. But then there were the trees on the mountain that Clay encountered in his dreams. Some trees had deep scars from what he surmised would have been carved by the claws of a bear or a mountain lion. The one thing Clay couldn't quite shake from his dreams about Mount Yah was the sense that someone or something was constantly watching him. It was as if he could feel the presence of whomever or whatever was there.

The dreams and the stories compelled Clay to go to the mountain. Mount Yah, he was convinced, was part of his destiny.

And so he continued to head West to the mysterious mountain to discover its treasure.

One day, Clay saw a mountain a little ways off in the distance. He and Virtue had been traveling for so long and had seen many mountains, especially the farther west they got. They had even passed over a few in their journey. Something inside him kept telling him that this mountain, could be the one he was looking for.

"Virtue, is this our mountain? I think it is, fella."

Hope rose in Clay's heart as he noticed the one defining characteristic that he had been told to look for: a river at the base of a mountain that runs between the mountain and a small town.

"You'll find a shallow river that's fanned out real wide. It sits there between the town and Mount Yah. The water of that river is sweet and cool. The town's called Settlersville," one of the travelers had said to Clay several days before.

And that's what Clay was eyeing—the wide river and small town. He was tempted to race Virtue the last few miles, but theirs had been a long journey. He knew it would be too much for his horse, pushing it hard this late in their travels could hurt Virtue, and Clay wasn't about to let that happen. The two of them had been through too much for that kind of nonsense.

Slowly but surely, Clay and Virtue made their way into Settlersville. Signs were above a few of the buildings. There was Baldwin's Barbershop & Bath, Mason's Mercantile, Jackson's Livery

& Stables, the Tall Saloon, Settler's Bank & Trust, and even a church with a bell in its steeple. These seemed to be the main buildings.

Clay noticed a small building that set away from everything else. It had a window with bars on its one side wall. That's the jail. I want to be sure to stay out of there, he thought to himself.

People were milling about, some working and others coming in and out of buildings. "Excuse me, boy," Clay heard a voice from inside the doorframe of the jail house, "I don't think I've seen you in these parts before."

A tall, broad shouldered cowboy stepped out from the jail house. The man had a square jaw and a thick mustache with a dark, stubbly beard growing in around it. The gleaming shine off his sheriff's badge caught Clay's eye.

"Well, no, sir, my name is Clay, and I'm just passing through," he responded nervously. Clay had heard stories about sheriffs in small towns like this. They would rough up anybody they didn't like and not think twice about it.

The man reached out his hand and with a firm handshake said, "Hi, Clay. My name is Sheriff Henry Billinger. Listen, I run a tight ship around here. If you steal, I'll jail you. If you pick a fight, I'll jail you. If you pull a gun on someone, I'll put a bullet in you before you have a chance to put your finger on the trigger."

Clay swallowed hard and then stuttered, "Y-y-yes, sir. I-I-I'm not looking to cause any trouble. I'm just looking for a homestead."

Sheriff Henry smiled a firm but warm smile, "Well, that's good to hear. You see, we love our little town, and I do everything in my power to make sure I guard our community. I hope you enjoy your time here."

Clay didn't really know much about the sheriff, but he figured the man probably was well respected in the community. Most good folk like knowing their sheriff is looking out for them anyway. He wondered if he would bump into anyone else in town.

Clay continued through the town. Occasionally, people smiled or nodded as he passed them. They seemed to be fairly nice folk, not wary of strangers, but something felt odd. There was a deep, unspoken caution that hung in the air. Though they appeared kind and friendly, the women still seemed scared and the men wounded. They weren't quite what he expected for blazing pioneers.

When Clay inquired about a place to stay by one of the passersby, he was pointed to the edge of town. He was told there was an abandoned homestead he could claim.

"Ain't nobody living out there now. And nobody has a claim on that property. I should know because I've been 'round these parts since forever," said the old man with a quirky grin on his face. "I'm Baldwin, and that's my barbershop right there. You just keep going as you are, and you'll find the cabin. The young man that lived there left some time ago. Twas in the night, if I recall, and that without warning. Well, that's neither here nor there. You just go settle yourself in there for now, for shelter."

22

"I really appreciate it, sir. I'll head right out that way. Me and the horse could use some rest," Clay said as he pressured Virtue's ribs with his legs, causing the horse to begin to move forward.

Strange, Clay thought, the former tenant's sudden departure didn't seem unusual to the old man. It was like he wrote it off as unimportant after he mentioned it to me. Must have been something to get the young fella to skedaddle out of there in the dark.

Clay made his way to the edge of town and found the homestead like he was told. It included an old cabin with no rooms. Inside was a makeshift kitchen and a crude fireplace. Clay didn't mind the old place because it was temporary. When he claimed his treasure, he knew he would build his own homestead.

As he began to clean the cabin, he found remnants of the previous tenant. He found an old knife, some broken plates, and one boot. Some tipped-over furniture and trash were left behind. Then, there were large claw marks on the walls and floors of the home. He couldn't help but think of the dreams he had had about the trees at Mount Yah. The claw marks on the walls and floors of the cabin left him with an eerie feeling, kind of made the hair on the back of his neck stand on end.

"Oh, well," Clay tried to comfort himself, "who knows what happened to the fella. This land is full of wild animals looking for a quick meal, so it's any wonder an animal could have got in here looking for food after the guy left. No concern of mine. It's late and time for bed. Tomorrow will be a full day. I best get some sleep."

He went right outside and tended to Virtue first. He did something his mother wouldn't have liked. Clay untied his horse and brought it right inside. There was no corral or barn to speak of, and he couldn't leave Virtue tied to a post, vulnerable to whatever roamed around these parts at night.

Next, Clay rolled out his blanket from his saddle and made his usual bed for the night. For the first time in a long while, he had a roof over his head. He was grateful for it, too.

Though Clay tried to rest, he kept seeing those claw marks in his mind. He didn't dare open his eyes for fear he would see the walls. He kept wondering whether the clawed walls had something to do with the former tenant's sudden departure. He simply couldn't shake the spooky feeling the marks gave him.

An hour or two went by, and Clay's tiredness grew louder than his thoughts. Soon, sleep caught up with him, and he stopped thinking about anything.

The next morning, Clay moved Virtue back outside and saddled the horse. Once the saddle was secure, he hopped on Virtue and began to ride back into town. He wanted to find the perfect plot of land upon which to build a home and start a family. That would require he find out the best way to get to Mount Yah. It wouldn't hurt to get to know the town a little more—and the people, too.

When Clay came into Settlersville, he decided to tie up Virtue and go his way around town by foot so that he could meet some of the locals. He walked to the one place where he knew he could find an older man who knew everything about the town: Baldwin's Barbershop & Bath. He noticed an old bearded man sitting outside and whittling on a small piece of wood. It wasn't Baldwin.

"Excuse me, sir, I'm looking for the path that leads to the top of Mount Yah. Can you point me in the right direction?"

The old man didn't look up or even acknowledge Clay's question. He kept carving the wood. It was the oddest thing. The old man's fingers were moving the wood about the knife rather than the other way around. He kept the knife stationary in his other hand all the while.

Clay stood there awkwardly. He was puzzled by what he saw the man doing. He was about to repeat what he had said but then decided to clear his throat instead. That seemed to prod the fella.

"Mount Yah," replied the old man in a deep, longing voice. It made Clay think he and the mountain were well acquainted. Besides, the old man leaned back in his chair and had a look on his face as if he were about to reminisce.

That's what he did as he then pointed his bony, crooked, right index finger toward the mountain he was staring at, "Atop Mount Yah is the most beautiful place known to man," he said nostalgically. "There's not a better place to start a family and build a life. They say that the water is as sweet as sugar cane and the ground is so fertile the harvest is triple what it is down here. The fruit is bigger, the crops grow taller, and the weather is like spring and fall all year long—"

"That's why I'm going, sir," Clay couldn't help but interrupt in his excitement. "How do I get up there?"

"You can't," said the old man.

"I can't? Why not?" Clay asked, taken back by the change in the old man's voice. It was if, all of the sudden, the man went cold. The hopeful reminiscence in his voice had been replaced with grave sadness.

"There is a bear that lives up there. Men have been trying to get up there for years, and few have made it. They have either been mauled or never came back down.

"He isn't like normal bears—he is evil. Men can't kill him, bullets do not faze him, and he has a particular craving for men's eyes and hearts. Some say he is Satan himself, but some say he is good, and if you take care of him, he will lead you to unimaginable treasure."

"Are you serious? This sounds just like an old fable born in the imagination of someone trying to keep people from the beauty of Mount Yah."

As soon as Clay finished speaking, the old man didn't say anything; he simply placed his knife and the piece of wood on his lap. Then, he pulled open his shirt and revealed four deep scars on his chest that went from his heart over his stomach and to his hip. The scars were thick and were purple.

Clay could tell that the attack almost claimed the man's life. That left Clay speechless. Even though he wanted to hear the story, he was too afraid to ask.

The old man then buttoned up his shirt, picked up his knife, closed it, picked up the piece of wood, placed both of them in his shirt pocket, stood up, and started into the shop. Just before he opened the barbershop door, he turned around and like a father would scold his son, he said, "It isn't worth it. Stay down here in Settlersville, ya hear?!"

The old man opened the door and walked in, but before he closed it, someone else came out of it and pulled it shut. It was Baldwin.

"Well, good morning, stranger. Did I ever get your name?"

"Morning, sir. No, you didn't. I'm Clay, and you're Baldwin, right?"

"That's right. Looks like you've been visiting with my oldest customer. He's probably the only man besides myself who knows this area like the back of his hand. His name's Adam. He's lived here forever, too."

"Yeah, I was asking him about Mount Yah—"

"Son, what are you wanting to know about Mount Yah? Betcha Adam told you not to go up there, didn't he? Well, you best ought to listen to him. He knows, trust me. He knows."

"I heard it from him. He told me not to go, but don't you worry. I can take care of myself. Made it all the way out here with nobody's help."

"Okay, Clay, you've been duly warned. Hope you found the homestead all right."

"Yes, Baldwin, thank you."

"Well, I better get back inside. I got customers waiting."

Clay just stood there a little while, thinking, What's wrong with these old men? They must be scared. A bear? Really? The story is obviously true because of the scars on Adam, but that was years ago. Surely the beast is dead by now.

A defiant determination came over him. He threw his shoulders back and walked up to Virtue, stabbing his boot into the horse's stirrup. Clay swung his leg over as he mounted his horse.

I didn't travel all the way out here just to settle in Settlersville. I'm gonna climb that mountain! No barber or scarred old man will stop me. But I sure hope the bear—if there is one—leaves me alone. I'm seeing too many signs for my comfort.

———

I place the book down, walk toward the mouth of the cave, and look out as the rain pounds on the outside world.

This is so much more than just a story. Settlersville?

And the mountain's name—Mount Yah—reminds me of the verse in the Bible, where it says, "Who shall ascend the hill of the Lord? He that has clean hands and a pure heart."

Right now, I know I can't ascend that hill. No, not me. My hands aren't clean, and my heart isn't pure.

That's exactly where I feel I am at right now. I have settled for pornography when God has called me up on the mountain.

I was not made to live and die in Settlersville. I was made to climb Mount Yah. But if I were Clay, I'd really be on the lookout for that bear. Those claw marks in his dreams, on the floor and walls of the cabin, and on old Adam's body give me the creeps.

I look back into the cave a little freaked out, very much aware of what could be lurking around me. I remind myself that nothing else is in the cave.

The next day, Clay rode Virtue back into town. Clay was about out of supplies. He needed oats for Virtue, food provision for himself, and after he saw the scars on that old man, he knew that he needed a gun with stronger stopping power. That led Clay to stop by Mason's Mercantile. He had some money of his own— money he had earned back home. But he also had some gold in a leather pouch that his parents had given him. They had handed it to him before he left to find the more, reminding him to be careful and not allow gold fever or love for money to find a place in his heart. He thought his parents would think he was being wise in purchasing a good weapon to keep himself safe. So he went forward with confidence to make a good trade, his gun and a little gold for a rifle and provisions.

Once inside the store, Clay's eyes soon landed on the exact weapon he required. It was a Hawken fifty-caliber rifle, strong enough to take down any mountain lion or bear. The proprietor noticed Clay ogling the rifle and said, "Hey there, young man, you spying out the Hawken? It's mighty powerful. It'll cost you a pretty penny."

"Yessiree, that's just the weapon I feel I'm needing. Would you be willing to take my gun here along with some gold for a trade? I also need some oil for my lamp and a few provisions. I'd appreciate your offering me a good price."

The proprietor said, "Sure, we can make a deal. I'm Mason, the owner. Mind my asking what you're planning on shooting?"

"Nice to meet you. I'm Clay. I'm heading up Mount Yah, and I want to be prepared for the—"

"Son," interrupted Mason the proprietor, "look here. You don't want to be going up there. There are some things that even a Hawken can't take out. I don't mean to be getting into your business, but—"

Clay didn't let the well-meaning man say another word, "Well, sir, you're right. You don't want to be getting into my business. Just leave well enough alone and give me the best price you can for my gun and let me know how much gold I need to add to it for these things I'm about to place on your counter."

Clay then proceeded to put some jerky, matches, ammunition, and oil on the counter. The proprietor began to make a tally of all the items on a piece a paper. When Clay had finished putting a few additional supplies on the counter for Mason to inventory, the proprietor wrote down an amount he would give for Clay's gun along with the total costs for the provisions. Mason handed the paper to Clay and said, "I'm sorry, Clay, I didn't mean to offend you. I trust you find these figures to be fair and honest."

"Here you go, Mason. This should cover it." Clay handed over his gun and some of the gold from his pouch. "Now, if you don't mind my asking, there is one other thing I need. Could you give me the directions to the mountain? I tried to get old Adam to tell me yesterday, but he wasn't having it. I'd appreciate it if you'd tell me."

"I guess you're set on going there. I wish you wouldn't, but I'll tell you how to find it." Walking over to the store's front window, Mason pointed toward a path leading away from the western edge of the town. "You follow that road there for a bit, cross the river—it's very shallow— and then you'll see a sign or two pointing you in the right direction. But, remember, I warned you not to go. Good luck, son."

Clay nodded his head appreciatively, walked back to the counter, and packed up his purchases. He headed in the direction of the door and heard Mason say under his breath, "I warned him. I've warned them all."

Clay didn't bother to say anymore to the man. He packed Virtue with all the wares he had purchased. He had to make one more stop to get hay and oats to feed Virtue. He made his way to Jackson's Livery to make arrangements.

When he was done, Clay came back to Virtue with a sack containing oats and hay. Climbing into his saddle and taking the reins, he said, "Clk-clk, let's go, Virtue. Time to find the more."

Clay headed toward the western edge of town. What he hadn't mentioned to anyone was that he couldn't wait another day. He had waited long enough already. He was bound and determined to get to Mount Yah. He basically had everything he needed anyway.

Clay road for over an hour when he found an old rotted-wood sign nailed to a tree. He could barely make out the words, "Mount Yah, beware." And there was a trace of a single arrow pointing down the path.

Clay smiled. Finally, he thought to himself, now I'm on the right path.

As he made his way forward, he found a Native American trader with all of his goods sprawled out on a handwoven blanket. He was set up by the river. The Native American man was tall with a stout muscular build. He had hair to his shoulders with a single feather tied in. Clay reached into his supplies and pulled out a pelt from a whitetail deer he had killed on his journey. Nothing the trader had spread out interested Clay, but he felt badly about looking at the man's wares without at least making an offer. That was when he noticed the hatchet attached to the trader's belt.

Clay motioned with his hand toward the hatchet, trying to gesture his way toward a deal.

The man shook his head from side to side, indicating he wasn't interested. The trader then reached in his horse's satchel and pulled out another hatchet. To Clay's surprise, the man agreed to the trade for this hatchet. The handle was strong and solid with beautifully etched designs. The blade was sharper than any blade Clay owned.

This will come in handy, especially if there is a giant bear on the mountain, Clay thought to himself. He meant it sarcastically.

"Thank you," Clay said with a smile that showed all his teeth. He slid the hatchet into his saddle bag, got back up on Virtue, and began his way across the river.

Everyone was right about one thing. The river was wide and, thankfully, shallow, too. Virtue had no trouble crossing the water because the deepest part only came up to the horse's knees.

Once across, Clay could see a path of sorts leading up the mountain. The trail was a bit overgrown, causing Clay to dismount and walk Virtue through the brush and thicket. As he began to get deeper and deeper into the wooded brush, he could hear his heart beat in his ears. Every so often either he or Virtue would brush against or step on a twig. Snap! Clay would hear the sound and immediately stop. Then, he would jerk his head around and raise his rifle as if on queue, sighting it toward the sound. After seeing nothing, he lowered his rifle, took his hat off, and wiped the sweat off his brow with his arm. He would start walking again. This was his pattern as he continued down the trail.

It didn't take too long before Clay's shirt was soaking wet. Why am I so scared? he thought. It's just a dumb story—a tall tale.

After an hour or so more, the burning of his legs from walking straight uphill caused him to forget the fear of the bear. He guessed that by tomorrow afternoon he would reach the summit. He was in the strange place where he was too far away to go back to town and too far down to reach the summit. He was smack in the middle.

Clay chose to bunk down, so he started looking for a good spot to camp. Anyway, he was tired, and he didn't want to push his horse anymore. He found an area near some large rocks. There were trees for shade and the rocks for protection. It looked suitable to him for a campsite. He built the fire next to the rocks to generate heat since it got pretty chilly at night. Clay pulled out some of the jerky he had traded for and began to bite into it. He soon finished his piece of jerky. He laid back against his saddle, feeling satisfied, and began to think about the top of the mountain and his new life. What will this place be like? Will I be the only one who lives there? Adam said it was the most beautiful place ever.

One thought led to another as Clay drifted off to sleep, his thoughts becoming nighttime dreaming of getting married and starting a family. He wanted to be a husband and a father, but when he was awake, the thought kind of scared him. What if he failed? What if he made a mistake and hurt his wife or child? His dreams attempted to answer those questions but then moved into another direction—that of life atop Mount Yah. Beautifully clear streams and smells of honeysuckle filled his senses as he dreamed of the mountaintop. Gorgeous vistas of Settlersville and beyond poured through his mind as he slept soundly.

Snap! Crunch! Klopp klopp klopp! Neigh! Neigh!

Clay was suddenly awakened by the sound of branches breaking and his horse going crazy. He quickly sat up in his daze and reached for his rifle right next to him. His fire was only a small pile of embers then, so he couldn't see very well. "Virtue, whoa there, fella," he said not seeing where the horse was or knowing what was happening.

Clay began to shake and sweat as he scanned his eyes rapidly from one side to the other. He was so shaken that his hair was standing on end like it did back at the cabin. After a minute, he realized the noise must have been a coyote spooking Virtue or something like that, so he sat back down against the saddle, still gripping his rifle with such intensity that his knuckles began to hurt.

In a few minutes, his breathing slowed back down, and his attention went to the fire. He added some fuel to it and began to listen to the sounds of the forest. Something moved by one of the trees. Clay could make out a silhouette. "Aw, it's just you, Virture." The horse seemed to be all right. "All's well, Virtue? Something got you all stirred up. Glad you're settled down, horse."

Clay's eyes chased over the shadows, still listening and looking to see if anything was out there. It was silent. Nothing moved. Whatever had caused such a fuss was over as quickly as it had begun.

Though Clay thought he was safe, he couldn't shake the feeling he was being watched, like he was being hunted. *Too many dreams and stories all scrambling around in my head. I'm getting too easily spooked like Virtue, that's for sure.* With that, he tried to get some more shut-eye before the sun would rise and the dew would begin to rest on the trees around him.

The following morning, Clay was glad the night was over. He figured he would have one more day of climbing before he reached the top of Yah.

———

Speaking of sleep, I check my watch and realize that it is getting pretty late. I am exhausted, but there is no way I can make it back to my camp in this weather. I'll just stay in the cave tonight and get some rest. I can use my pack as a pillow, and I have plenty of wood to keep me warm through the night.

I can feel sleep coming to my body while I begin wondering what tomorrow will look like for Clay and for me as well.

CHAPTER 3

THE CAVE

The cold, hard floor of the cave awakens me from my short-lived sleep. I wake up in a confused, slightly afraid daze, wondering where I am and how I got here. The fire that once kept me warm and in the light is simply a heap of dust and ashes. The darkness is thick and tangible. I need to get my fire going again.

I quickly grab some small twigs, pine thistles, and branches from the pile I found yesterday and throw them on the ash pile. I then get on my knees and begin to start a fresh fire. To my relief, everything is dry enough and easily kindles. I have a couple of hours before the sun comes up, and I am eager to find out what happens to Clay.

"Got me hooked, this story has. It looks like I won't be getting my beauty rest tonight," I say aloud to myself. Hearing my own voice in my aloneness spooks me a little.

I rip open a Cliff bar and continue to read.

—→

After a quick breakfast, Clay dumped some dirt on his fire to make sure it was done burning and packed up his belongings on the back of his horse, readying himself to set off again. The way was narrow and rough. The trail seemed a little washed out from a previous rain, but Clay's excitement for reaching the top kept him pushing on.

As he was following the path, he noticed something glistened. It shone from a higher point on the mountain, a little ways below the summit. Clay stopped to make it out and noticed the glistening thing actually came from what looked like a cave above some bluffs. Off to the right of the cave was a cascading waterfall.

From what Clay could see, he would have to get off the trail to get over to the bluffs and then climb them to ascend to a ledge that led to the opening of the cave. Clay knew he didn't have time to waste and needed to stay on the beaten path, but there was this curiosity in him that he couldn't quiet. He had to know what was in there. He had to see it for himself. *What if it's gold hidden in there? Besides, I've been walking for hours and could use a rest.*

Clay tied Virtue to a nearby tree and set off toward the cave. Since he didn't think it would take him too long and he needed his hands available to do some climbing, Clay left his rifle in its holster on his saddle. He did grab his tomahawk and attached it to his belt, in case there was an unexpected visitor in the cave. Then, he began to make his way to the bluffs.

Clay arrived at the base of the bluffs to find a pretty steep rock face. He turned around and looked back at his horse still tied to the tree. Something was gnawing him in his gut. He felt uneasy because he had already been away from Virtue for too long. And when he had looked back, he recognized he was farther away from Virtue than he thought he should be. The cave had seemed a good deal closer to the path while he was on it. *Maybe I should head back? But I'm so close to the waterfall. It would be great to get a taste of that sweet water Adam talked about. And what if there's gold? I just have to see if the gold is here—if it's what's shining out from the cave.* Clay felt torn.

Convincing himself he could hurry it up and Virtue would be okay under that tree, he proceeded to climb. He ended up scaling the rock face that was about ten feet high. He made it up the first eight feet without too much of a problem, but he would have to pull himself up the final few feet. Gripping into the rock outcrops with his hands and pushing off the face with his feet, he hauled himself up until his head popped up over the rock ledge and he was looking directly into the pitch black entrance to the cave. Lugging himself up the rest of the way, he was able to crawl over to his left—to the waterfall. Clay ducked his head under it, allowing the cool water to run down the back of his head and stream down off his face. He licked his lips, eager to get a taste.

"I need to get a good swig of this water. All I can taste is the dust of the trail mixed with a lot of salty sweat. I wonder if this becomes the river that runs from Mount Yah and fans out below, where me and Virtue crossed?" he asked aloud. Cupping his hands and catching some of the water, Clay took a big drink. As the water filled his mouth, he immediately spat it out. It was bitter. Disgusted, he jumped up and backed away from the waterfall, almost falling backwards off the ledge. Clay was so angry he almost forgot why he came.

"If Adam and those other travelers were wrong about the water up here, maybe I better go back down to Settlersville!" He turned around and sat on the ledge, ready to lower himself down the rock face. Then, he remembered the gold and the shiny thing he had seen from the path.

Resting on the ledge for a few minutes more, Clay looked down toward the path to find his horse, but he couldn't see Virtue anywhere. Confident he was simply overlooking it and sure of his ability to get back to the path later on, he stood himself up, turned toward the opening of the cave, and began to walk into it to have a look around.

At first, Clay couldn't see much because of coming into the dark from the bright outside, but his eyes began to adjust after a few minutes. It wasn't long before Clay could make out the crystalline walls. The cave was the most beautiful thing he had ever seen. He noticed a golden seam running through the crystal and even up in the rock above. He was in awe of what he discovered. With the amount of gold he was seeing in this cave, he would be able to build an amazing life! His mind raced toward the future—to the large house and the acres of land for cattle. *Shoot, I'll be able to buy all of Settlersville if I want,* he mused, *or maybe even Mount Yah!*

Pulling his tomahawk from his belt, Clay swung it and hacked at the walls. The pounding resounded throughout the cave, returning to him and piercing his ears, but he didn't care. He just kept at it until he thought he heard something amid his banging. He stopped for a moment, listened, but heard nothing. So, he started striking the walls again to see if he could get some of the gold from the seam.

Originally distracted by the beauty of the cave, Clay had never even thought of making sure he was alone in there. But he started to wonder when once again he thought he heard something. He stopped cutting at the cave wall and immediately heard, *Grrrr. Grrrr.* It was a deep growl that reverberated in his chest. He froze.

———

Whirrffftt! I slam the journal shut. I don't read another line.

That's it. I can't take it. I am in a cave, and this guy ends up in a cave. He's hearing things. If I read anymore, I think I'm going to start hearing things. This is really starting to freak me out.

I inch closer toward the mouth of the cave, just in case. But I can't put away the journal. I have to open it. I have to find out what happens. "I must be some kind of sick dude," I speak out loud so as to at least make myself feel like someone is there in the cave with me—someone I can trust and talk to. "I can't put away porn at home, and I can't put down a book that's downright creeping me out, scaring me to death. I'm really messed up."

Opening the journal, I finger through the pages, looking for where I left off.

———

A deep growl thundered through the cave then suddenly ended.

"Welcome," said a deep raspy voice.

Clay jumped back and instinctively raised his tomahawk in the air. "Who's there?" exclaimed Clay, as he took a step back, keeping his tomahawk raised above his head.

"The owner of this cave and a friend."

"Show yourself! Where are you?"

"You cannot see me, and I don't think you would want to."

Clay was really confused, scared, and strangely interested to see who or what it was. The voice sounded evil yet inviting. It was odd.

"You may take as much gold as you like, my young friend, for I see that you are a young boy who seeks to become a man. In this very cave, many boys have become men through the riches that I give."

"Well, thank you, that's mighty generous of you," Clay tried to sound friendly though he was very reluctant to believe the voice to be trustworthy, and he didn't like being called a *young boy*.

"I just want to tell you that your first visit is free. After this, I will require payment," the voice seemed closer then.

"How much payment?" asked Clay, really looking hard to see who was speaking to him.

"That is for another time," said the voice. "Now, take as much as you please."

"This will probably be the only time you see me. I just need this one trip."

"Of course," the voice said as if it were smirking.

Clay went back to work striking the wall with his tomahawk. Chunks of crystalized rock broke free and rattled down to the cave's floor. Clay kept at it for a while, making several small piles along the wall's face. He wasn't prepared for all the gold he was going to bring back with him, so he filled his pockets and took his shirt off and made a makeshift bag to put his minings into. Even with the small amount that he took, he knew it would be enough to build a home and buy a significant tract of land. He surmised that he would have what he needed to start a good life.

Making his way out of the cave, Clay looked over his shoulder one more time, his eyes squinting toward the recesses of the inside. He was looking for the form of the mysterious voice, the owner of the cave.

"Remember," grunted the razor-like voice—from where?—Clay didn't know, "you are never to tell anyone about this, and next time you come, I will require payment."

Clay grinned cunningly and nodded his head. *With all of this gold, I will never have to return. I've bested this fella for sure,* he thought.

When Clay walked onto the ledge outside the cave, he was startled to see how late it had become. The sun was on its way down. "How long was I in there? It seemed like an hour at the most."

Quickly, Clay sat down on the ledge and pushed himself gently down the side, turning to face the rock face as he went. He climbed down the bluffs, carefully finding his footing as he descended. He didn't want to lose an ounce of his gold.

By the time Clay got back to the path, the sunset was just about complete. He knew his horse was thirsty and felt badly for leaving Virtue tethered without water for such a long time. He continued on the path persuading himself as he walked that his horse would be all right. *After all,* he reasoned, *Virtue will have all the water and oats it needs very soon. I've got the gold I need to give Virtue all it wants!*

Arriving at the tree where he thought he had tied his horse, Clay's heart suddenly sank. Virtue was gone! And with it, all of the provisions and supplies Clay had in the world.

Clay desperately looked from tree to tree, hoping he was wrong, hoping he had mistaken the spot, but then he saw the horse's lead was at the base of the tree right in front of him. That wasn't the only thing he noticed, for carved into the tree's trunk were three distinct claw marks.

"Oh, no, the bear!" Clay panicked. It felt as if the wind was knocked out of him. "That bear devoured Virtue! I left it tied up, and it was just an easy meal." Clay's eyes watered up as he realized his stupid mistake. He began to regret leaving the path even though he did get all the gold.

Then, he remembered the reason why he was up there in the first place. He had believed his destiny was atop Mount Yah, up on its summit, and the gold seemed worthless, insignificant, in comparison. If he had only stayed the course, he would have already been atop the mountain.

Clay scanned the grounds around him for some of his belongings, thinking something might have fallen off during the attack, but all he found in the encroaching darkness was an old cup and some cooking utensils. He did see tracks leading away from that spot, some bear and some horse.

Maybe Virtue isn't dead. Maybe it's just lost, Clay thought to himself. The thought appeared to relieve his heavy heart.

—

Man, that's a bummer about his horse, Virtue. But with that gold, he can buy a million horses. I just want him to stay far away from that cave and that guy up there. And keep away from any bears!

I can't help but look around my surroundings to see if I have any unwanted guests. Seeing nothing or no one else, I stand up and stretch. Sitting for so long is making my legs cramp. I take a few steps toward the diminishing supply of wood, bend down, pick up a few smaller pieces, stand back up, and go stoke the fire with one of them. Then, I drop both pieces of wood in the fire. It's good and lit now.

I reach into my pack and pull out some beef jerky and my bottled water. I close my pack and then sit down, scooting my rear and back into the pack against the wall. I return to poor Clay who has lost his Virtue.

Clay stood there a little while longer. Then, he looked up the narrow path, the one that wound its way up the mountain. And he looked down the path in the opposite direction, back to Settlersville. He then decided within himself that he couldn't make it all the way to the top without his belongings, provisions, or his horse. In that moment, Clay realized that he might as well hike down to Settlersville, use his gold to buy a new horse, and get supplies to replenish what was missing.

Having been very excited initially, Clay began his long journey back down the mountain defeated by the knowledge that he never got to the top of Mount Yah. He couldn't help but feel shame as he walked down. He didn't really know why, but it kept growing and growing. He tried to encourage himself, "It's easier walking downhill anyway, and as I go the path seems to get broader and broader." But no matter how hard he tried, the aching feeling inside only got worse.

When Clay stopped to sleep for the night, he was able to start a fire with some flint from his pocket and some brush and twigs he had gathered. There, he stared at the gold. It was the only way he found any comfort. He was grateful to at least have the gold and greatly anticipated getting to town and placing it in the bank. The sting of losing Virtue lessened a little the more he thought about what the gold would buy him. *In a way, Virtue was a necessary sacrifice in order to become a man,* Clay thought. *Now, I can build a house, start a family, and buy ten horses if I want.* He worked hard to rationalize the loss away—maybe a little too hard.

CHAPTER 4

THE FAKE

The next morning, Clay plucked some berries off a nearby bush and made his way back down the mountain. He came to the river and remembered how excited he was when he first crossed it while riding Virtue. The memory stung.

It had been a long, grueling walk. Clay had time to search his soul. He rehearsed his parents' warning when they had given him the pouch of gold. He knew better than to let the love of money or gold fever get the better hand. That memory hurt, too.

He didn't remember anyone ever warning him about the bewitching attraction something shining and beautiful could have on a man—the luring curiosity the appearance of beauty could generate. But it didn't matter anyway. It was too late. He had been captivated. The only thing at this point offering him any consolation was the value of the gold for his future. Driving him forward was the thought of cashing the gold in at the bank and planning the future it would buy him.

When he arrived back in town, he found an old chicken feed bag that had been thrown away and put the gold he had in it. This allowed him to empty the gold from his shirt and out of his pockets. He put his shirt back on, buttoned it up, and tucked it in his pants. At least he'd be fully clothed when he got back into town. He then continued on into Settlersville.

Clay looked a sight, but he didn't care. What he was carrying with him was all that mattered. Though he didn't look like it, he was the richest man in town. He even grinned at the people he passed though they seemed amused by his appearance. *If they only knew what I had in this bag,* he thought.

Settler's Bank & Trust was busy that afternoon. Clay opened the door and walked right in, the bell rang, and everyone turned around and looked at him. He then went and stood in the nearest line and stayed there, feeling out of place in his filthy, sweat-stained clothes.

"Next!" shouted the old man behind the counter. The teller had a visor cap on, small glasses that rested on his nose, and a clean, white, stiffly starched, buttoned-down shirt.

Clay walked up and placed his chicken feed bag on the counter.

"Well, what's this, boy? We don't take chicken feed, just money," the old man snapped at him, trying to embarrass Clay with his wit.

The bank was a small building with everyone in one room, so everyone heard what the teller had said to Clay. Clay even heard several people chuckle. All eyes were on him and the teller. Clay was glad, so now he could make a fool of this old man. If he wanted to, he would buy this bank with all the money in it! He'd show them all.

Clay then grabbed a big handful of the gold and threw it on the table with little nuggets and chunks spreading everywhere. He wanted to make a statement, allowing the gold to speak for itself. And it seemed to work because the teller's mouth dropped open and an audible gasp filled the room. The next thing Clay knew was people came running over to see the gold that lay on the table.

"You might want to call the bank manager over," Clay said with a smile, trying to put the old teller in his place.

The teller called for the bank manager, and both bankers began to inspect the gold as onlookers spoke in hushed voices.

Clay was very careful not to tell them about the exact location, but he did tell them it was on a mountain in the distance.

Suddenly, the bank manager and the teller began to laugh hysterically, and several of the people joined them.

"What's so funny?" Clay asked, seeming to be the only man in the room not to get the joke.

Everyone just kept laughing, and in between gasps of air, Clay could make out a couple of words.

"It's—er—ha, ha, ha—fake!" the manager exclaimed with tears starting to run down his cheeks. He and all the others couldn't stop laughing.

"No, no, you're mistaken," said Clay.

The bank manager then began to scratch one of the large chunks with a letter opener, causing the gold color to disappear. All that was left was a chunk of rock.

"But, but—" Clay said, blushing in embarrassment.

"Get out of here, boy, and take your chicken feed with you!"

The teller cackled as Clay snatched the bag from the old man's hand and stormed furiously out the door. He was so angry that big tears were beginning to well up in his eyes. He fought with every ounce of his being not to shed a tear. That would just make them laugh even harder.

As his hand reached for the door knob, a raspy voice echoed over the laughter of the people. "Quiet!" It was as if the air was sucked out of the room. Everyone went silent. As Clay turned around, he saw Adam, the scarred man he had talked to in front of Baldwin's Barbershop & Bath.

"He's not the only one in this town who has been deceived by the gold of that mountain, is he? I bet there are a few of us in this room with fake gold in our sock drawers. Leave the boy alone." Everyone's heads dropped, their eyes then fixed on the floor—all but Clay's, that is.

Clay made eye contact with the man and gave him a nod. He might not have said it, but Adam could see Clay was grateful for the kindness.

I can't help but think of that story in the Bible. It's the one where the woman was caught in the act of adultery in John 10. She must have been embarrassed and exposed in front of all the religious hot-shots of her day. That's how I feel after I stumble and look at pornography. The shame of being exposed causes me to retreat further into hiding. She deserved death and embarrassment according to the law, but thankfully for her and Clay, they had someone step in and defend them.

Lord, I feel like I'm surrounded by my enemies with stones raised, ready to throw. I need Your defense, Jesus. Like Clay and the woman, I need You to intervene.

Tears begin too well up into my eyes as I try to focus back on Clay's story. *Must be the dust in the cave,* I try to convince myself.

All the way home, Clay heard the jeering laughter in his mind. He couldn't shake it.

When he arrived back to his cabin, he kicked open the door and threw the bag against the wall, causing the contents of the bag to spill all over the floor.

"Blast! I lost Virtue over something fake! It wasn't even fool's gold. And I never got to the top of Mount Yah. I got tricked!" hollered Clay. He backed himself into a corner in his cabin and slowly slid himself down to the floor. He sorely wept in his anger and frustration.

Finding and bringing home the gold was supposed to make him a man, but all it did was reaffirm that he was a boy. One look at a shimmering object pulled him off the trail to his destiny, separated him from Virtue forever, and made him the laughingstock of some two-bit town.

Later that night, as he lay in bed, he could not stop hearing the laughter of those men in the bank. His anger burned more and more at them. "There has to be gold up there," he reasoned, "that old man in the cave just put this fake stuff in there to keep people away. Tomorrow, I am going back up there and getting the real gold!"

Clay tried to calm himself and get some sleep, but it was awfully difficult. He lay there for hours before the emotion drained out of him. Completely wrung out, he fell asleep.

The next morning, the sun peeked through the base of the door of the cabin, and soon the entire cabin was lit by it. Clay woke up to the sunshine with renewed vigor. He was determined to get the gold and show everybody that he could do it. He picked up what few belongings he had left and walked out the door.

Fortunately, he took the money he had in his pocket and tucked it away in his boot for safe keeping. His first order of business would be to go to the mercantile and get some provisions to help him on his journey. By then, everyone in town would know what had happened to him. Mason and Adam would tell him that they had warned him. He dreaded running into them, but there was no way around it.

Firmly setting his jaw and walking with his back as stiff as a wrought-iron post, Clay walked into the mercantile, right up to Mason, and with no small talk said, "I need some provisions. I have some money to use."

Mason had heard about Clay's misfortune. Feeling sorry for him and knowing how badly bruised the young man's ego must have been in that moment, he honored Clay by asking no questions and leaving well enough alone.

"Clay, you just put what you want on the counter, and I'll figure out what you owe."

The two men exchanged the goods for the money. Clay was grateful to have been treated respectfully. He was relieved.

"May I leave the provisions here for a few minutes?" Clay asked.

"Sure, I'll keep an eye on your things for you," Mason replied.

"Thank you, sir," Clay said as he walked out the door. He went to the livery next door and purchased a mule. It was what he could afford to replace Virtue. And then he went and tied it outside the store.

Clay went back into Mason's Mercantile and picked up his new shovel, pickaxe, lantern, matches, and other provisions he had purchased. He took it all outside and packed it on the mule. After getting everything set, he headed toward the mountain to get his gold.

Clay thought of the last time he saw Virtue. He wouldn't make the same mistake he did last time, so he meant to take the mule as far as he could with him. At least this time, he would leave his animal off the path, somewhat hidden. And having his stuff closer to him would help him be able to bring more of the tools he needed to retrieve the gold.

CHAPTER 5

THE RETURN

Clay camped where he did the first night he was on the Mount Yah trail, up against a group of rocks. Once again, he made a campfire and prepared his bed.

The night was uneventful, unlike that first night with Virtue getting all spooked. Clay appreciated the fact because it meant he was able to rest up for the hard work before him.

Early the next day, Clay put out the already fading fire. He packed up his stuff on the mule's back, and the two walked toward the bluffs. He found a good spot to tie the mule. It was halfway between where they had camped and the bluffs. The area was thick with trees. Clay felt it would keep the mule hidden away from anyone, especially seeing it was far enough away from the mountain's trail.

Taking the pack off the mule and tying it onto his back, Clay made his way to the base of the bluffs. He had a lantern, pickaxe, and shovel with him, and his hunting knife and tomahawk were attached to his belt. It was a hard climb up the rock face this time. The added weight made it more difficult, but once Clay reached the ledge and pulled himself up to the opening of the cave, he wasted no time in taking his lantern from his pack and lighting it, and then marching right into the darkness.

"Hello?!" he yelled, listening to his voice echo through the cave.

No answer.

The crazy owner must be out hunting. Maybe if I hurry, I can leave before he returns. He owes me after he embarrassed me in town with that fake stuff. This should still be considered free and not require payment, Clay thought to himself as he lifted his lantern and began to walk deeper into the cave.

He had done a lot of thinking over the past twenty-four hours, specifically about what the owner must have done to him. Clay figured the man put the fake stuff at the front of the cave and kept the real stuff hidden deeper into it. He went back a good three-hundred feet and found a spot, raised his pickaxe, and struck the beautiful walls of the cave.

Though he still wasn't sure if what he was piling up was gold, he kept at it, filling two bags at a time and then lowering them down the outside bluff so as to have as much out of the cave as he could in case the owner showed up. He felt he had a better chance that what he had gathered was real gold because it seemed heavier and the color didn't scratch off.

Clay realized as he worked that he loved being in this cave. In this cave, he was the richest, the most powerful man in the world! All the gold he could take was right in front of him. It made him feel larger than life.

After lowering the third and fourth bags down, Clay made his way back into the cave to fill up his final bags. Each time he had gone back in, he had moved a little farther past where he had been the time before. This last time, he went pretty far back into the cave. Raising his pickaxe over his head, he thought he heard something moving behind him.

"Welcome back, my young friend. It didn't take as long I expected for you to return," the owner's voice bounced off the cave walls, amplifying its sound.

Startled, Clay spun around trying to locate the voice and asked, "How long have you been there?"

"Long enough to determine the price of your payment," the owner said resolutely.

"I don't owe you anything because the gold you gave me last time was fake. I've come back for the real thing!" Clay's anger could be heard in his tone.

"The real thing is surely in here. But it is deeper within this cave, and I am the only one who can take you there."

Clay grabbed his lantern, the two sacks, his pickaxe, and said, "Show me the way." He squinted but could barely make out the form of the man who was somewhere in the shadows ahead of him. From what he saw, the man couldn't be much taller than himself.

"Follow me," the owner said.

Clay headed in the owner's direction. The man managed to keep a ways off. Clay picked up his pace to try to shorten the distance between them, but it was if the man somehow knew it and kept apace of Clay, staying just far enough away for Clay not to get a good look at him. From time to time, the owner would tell Clay to follow the sound of his voice.

I don't know what the big deal is—why doesn't he let me see him? He must be disfigured or something.

The air was getting colder as the two descended into the cave. Clay noticed a distinct smell that became more pronounced the further back he went. He recognized the smell. It was the smell of death.

There must have been an animal that came in and died, or maybe this man lives in here and kills animals for food, leaving their carcasses to rot, he reasoned.

Either way, Clay didn't care what it smelled like as long as he got some of the real gold.

"Here we are, young man," the voice said.

Clay raised his lantern and looked around. They had arrived at what seemed to be the end of the cave. It was a big cavern with a much higher ceiling than where he had been mining. There were huge stalactites hanging down. Clay lifted his lantern up to get a better look at the rock formation above him. Casting the light across rock ceiling and back around to the ground, he noticed the entire cavern was nothing but gold—the ground, the walls, and the ceiling—everything! Gold was everywhere! And the color was brilliant.

Clay's eyes brightened as he gazed at the beauty of the gold. He brought the lantern back down to his side and then dropped his two bags and pickaxe, awestruck by what he saw.

"How much?" Clay asked, still staring at the gold all around him.

"The payment isn't much," the owner responded. "It will be well worth what you receive here. Once you pay, you can have as much gold as you like."

"I'll do anything," Clay said, looking in the direction of the owner's voice, still only able to see the shadow of the man. "How much?"

"Just your heart."

"My heart?" Clay asked, stunned by the man's answer. He wondered, *What an odd price to pay. Could he be joshing me?* Clay wasn't sure.

"Just give me your heart, and all of this gold will be yours. You don't really need your heart to be a man. No, you just need the beauty of this gold. As you can see, it not only gives you pleasure to behold it, but it will buy you pleasure, happiness, and all the land you can imagine. Me, I only need your heart."

After that, Clay realized the man was serious. His mind began to race, *How did I get into this mess? What am I doing? What about Mount Yah, my family, my dreams, my destiny?* Clay couldn't believe he had allowed himself to get so deep in the cave and so caught up in the gold that he had forgotten where he came from and what the reason was for his coming to the mountain in the first place. He finally began to think clearly again, but that was only temporary, for his eyes caught sight of the dazzling gilded cavern. Transfixed by its brilliance, Clay grew intoxicated by the idea of the gold and what it offered him. Yet something was telling him he needed to get out of there while he still could. *But how?*

"You know, on second thought, that is too steep of a price for me. I guess I could have all of those things without my heart, but I would be numb. I wouldn't be able to enjoy them. I'd be a dead man walking, right? Nah, I can't do it."

As he said it, a guttural growl came from the darkness. Clay quickly turned his lantern in the direction of the noise. As he did, the man's figure slowly began to come into view. Watching closely and wanting to finally see the face of the voice he had been listening to—the face of the man who had tricked him—Clay's eyes were riveted on the emerging figure. What he saw in slowly ticking seconds took his breath away.

Appearing eye level at first, suddenly, the form rose five feet above Clay's head. He had to lift up his lantern and eyes to see it. The figure was huge. The man was a giant, and he was hairy!

Wait a minute! Clay's mind rushed to catch up with what he was seeing. Rapidly moving his head from side to side as if to deny what he saw, Clay couldn't keep his thoughts inside anymore. He blurted out, "You're no man. You're—you're a—you're a bear! Oh, no! *You're the bear!*"

"*Grrr! Grrr!*" The bear let out a howl that was more like a prehistoric roar. It shook the walls of the cavern and caused Clay's ears to ring in pain.

As if that weren't enough for the young man to handle, the hot putrid breath of the bear blew upon Clay's face. It was mixed with the spray of saliva. Clay was paralyzed with fear, causing him to fall back like a falling tree blasted over by a violent gust of wind.

Somehow, Clay's feet moved intuitively to stabilize him, but it was to no avail. Something was on the ground, and his feet kept slipping and tripping over whatever it was. He couldn't help but slam down to the ground as his feet went out from under him.

Instinct kicked in. Clay tried to stand back up so he could run. Using his hands to push himself up, his eyes landed on what had tripped him up—bones! The light from Clay's lantern that was now on the ground behind him lit the floor, revealing the hundreds, if not, thousands of human bones and skulls in piles pushed back against the one side of the cave. They were just outside the cavern at the end of the tunnel.

How did I not see those before? Clay was puzzled. *That gold—I must have been distracted by that gold and by my trying to get a good look at the owner when I was following him down here!*

"Your heart belongs to *me*!" snarled the bear.

"No, never!" Clay managed to scream back, fighting the fear that was gripping him spirit, soul, and body.

In anger, the bear swung its massive paw directly at Clay's head and slashed him from his forehead down to the top of his cheekbone. Blood gushed from Clay's wound, down his face, and onto his neck. As the bear raised its other paw to deliver its final blow, Clay ducked away and began running toward the cave's entrance. He ran as fast as he could until he saw the mouth of the cave. He almost flew out of the opening and managed to slide on his bottom down the ten-foot rock face. The rocks were tearing into his jeans and embedding themselves in the flesh on his legs and backside.

Finally, Clay's feet hit the base of the bluff, and he kept running, even leaving his bags of gold behind. He didn't stop until he made it back to where he had tied up his mule.

His mind was careening out of control. It flashed back to what had happened to his horse—to the horse and bear tracks near the tree and to the three claw marks on the tree—"That bear killed Virtue!" the words burst from Clay's mouth. That's when it all began to make sense to him. But he didn't have time to stand there and think. No, he wasn't safe as yet.

Clay looked back to see if he was being chased by the bear but saw no trace of the monster. He quickly untied his mule and pulled it down the hill until they both collapsed next to the river. He had pushed himself and the mule so hard that he forgot about his wounds. The adrenaline in his body kept him from paying attention to his own pain. The blood had slowed to more of a crusted oozing during his escape. Dried blood, however, sealed shut the eyelid of his right eye.

Clay slowly crawled over to the stream and could see his reflection in the water. What he saw startled him. He had three deep claw marks on his face that ran over his eye. Maybe the adrenaline was wearing off or maybe it simply was the fact that Clay could now see the extent of his injuries. Either way, he began to feel the stinging pain.

Nevertheless, the young man plunged his face into the cold stream to wash the blood off and bring comfort to his wounds. When he pulled his face out of the water, he pulled his eyelid up and found that he still had his eye and could see out of it. His sight was blurry. That was all.

Clay began to realize that the bear was aiming for his eyes. That bear, as Adam had warned him, did have "a craving for men's eyes and hearts." He thought back to how the bear asked for his heart for payment of the gold and how it had attacked him, remembering both swipes at him were intentionally headed for his eyes. The bear must have figured that, if it could get his eyes, it could easily get his heart.

No longer caked in dried blood, Clay's eye was still shut; in fact, it was swollen shut. He got up from the stream and went over to a nearby tree, leaning against it before deciding to go ahead and sit down to rest. The terror of the experience began to replay in his mind, causing his eyes to fill with tears. The tears caused his wounds to hurt even more, making him feel the hurt of the experience. He took a deep breath so as to settle himself, but when he exhaled, everything came barreling out of him. He sobbed, unable to then catch his breath, and he kept crying until there was nothing left in him.

Look at you, he was disgusted by his inability to contain his emotions. *You're nothing more than a little boy crying in the woods by himself. You will never be a man unless you get that gold.*

Clay felt as if he always had two voices in his head wrestling to be heard. One told him to be a man, to act like a man, to look like a man, and to lust like a man. It despised weakness. The other seemed more rational because it put up cautions, warning Clay for his own good. That inner voice won out for the moment.

What am I thinking? Get the gold? Go back? How could I ever go back and face that bear again? This time I was lucky, but who knows what would happen to me if I went back in there with that monster!

The more Clay sat there, the more his mind wanted to throw caution to the wind and go and get the gold. It was as if the gold attached itself to his heart and mind. He had to go back one more time and get as much of that gold as possible. The battle began in his mind. One minute he firmly would plant his feet and determine he would never step foot back in that forsaken cave, but then he would remember the adrenaline rush he had had as he had harvested the gold from the cave. The feeling he had had, that he was the most powerful person in the world, *That's worth it all! I've got to experience that feeling of the more!* He convinced himself what he had to do.

—➤

This guy is crazy! Going back to the cave after he almost died? Really? No way I would ever go back in there. He must have a death wish.

As I begin to think about it more, I realize I have no room to talk. *How many times have I told God, "Never again!" only to go back? It's like what Proverbs 26:11, "As a dog returns to its vomit, so a fool repeats his folly."*

It's as if my mind shuts down when I'm being tempted. I try to scream to myself, "Wake up! You told God that you wouldn't go back!" Then, like a hypnotized man, I turn on the computer and type in that website.

"Waitress, one slice of humble pie, please," I say, realizing I'm no different than Clay in his pursuit of the more.

—➤

Just one more time. That's it. This will be my last time. Clay was firm in his decision. He was going to be a man and get his revenge on that bear, but more importantly, he was going to get that gold no matter what it took.

Clay gathered his belongings together. He set up camp right there by the river. It was far enough away from Mount Yah so that he didn't feel threatened by an attack from the bear.

That afternoon, as the sun was going down, he began to make a plan on how to get the gold. He thought about it as he made his campfire. *Maybe I can barter with the bear? He seemed to only get angry when I didn't go along with his chosen payment. I remember what Adam said. He said that some people claim the bear is good if you take care of him. Well, that's what I'll do. I'll take care of him!*

Just then, he heard a noise coming from the woods. Quickly, Clay stood up and grabbed a broken branch that was resting on a rock beside him. "Get back! Get back!" he cried as the figure came into the light.

"Whoah, now, I'm your friend," said the man as he became visible. The man was in his thirties and was larger than most men Clay had met. He was clothed in animal skins and had long hair that went to his shoulders and a beard that hung down to his chest. He had a feather tied in his hair like the Native American trader, and the claws of a bear hung around his neck. Clay could tell that this man had seen many battles and was quite the warrior, yet his eyes were tender and full of compassion. Clay noticed the man had a

Native American tomahawk attached to his belt on one side and a large staghorn knife attached to the other. The man had with him a large white horse that was carrying his gear, and he had a nice rifle in the holster on his saddle.

"Who are you?" said Clay defensively, still holding the branch in the air.

"My name's Joshua, and you can lower your weapon. I'm not here to fight with you. I'm just passing through and looking for a hot fire to get warmed by."

Clay then realized how dumb he must have looked with a branch above his head as his only weapon. He lowered it but didn't let it go.

Joshua then noticed the blood on Clay's shirt and the wounds on his head. "Are you okay?"

"Yeah, yeah. I was attacked by a mountain lion earlier while hunting. It's not a big deal."

"That was one big mountain lion," Joshua responded with a chuckle. He then reached into his saddlebag and pulled out a metal tin. "Here," Joshua said, throwing the tin to Clay, "rub this balm on your wounds. It will cause them to heal quickly. What's your name?" the man asked.

"Clay," he responded while gently applying the balm to his wounds.

The balm was thick with a sweet smell that he had never smelled before. As soon as he put it on his wounds, he could feel the stinging pain go away, and the swelling seemed to go down as well.

"Wow, what is this stuff?"

"It comes from the fruit of a tree on Mount Yah," Joshua responded, looking at the mountain in the distance.

"You have been to Mount Yah?" Clay asked.

"Been there, I live there!"

"What? Are you serious? What's it like up there?"

"There is no place like it. Words can't do it justice. Why don't you come up there and see for yourself?"

Clay had a deep longing to go to the top of Mount Yah, but before he could say *yes*, he was reminded of the cave. He sat down against the rocks, settling into his bedding.

"I can't. I got some things I've got to do down here."

"What do you mean you can't? I'll lead you up there and help put you on the finest plot of land on the mountain."

The best land for free? How? No, it's too good to be true. Just like the bear in the cave, there must be a catch. He's probably trying to lure me up there to enslave me or something.

"And whatever you have to handle down here, I can handle for you," Joshua responded. "No matter how big and intimidating those mountain lions are."

"You know what? I don't need your help. I can do this myself. Now, if you don't mind, I have a big day ahead of me tomorrow, and I need some rest."

"Are you sure—"

"Goodnight, and thank you for the medicine," Clay interrupted as he lay back and pulled his blanket over himself.

"It was nice meeting you, Clay, and my offer still stands," Joshua said as he untied his horse and walked into the wilderness.

As the sound of the hooves grew faint in the distance, Clay began to dream of the gold hidden in the darkness again. It was all a mystery why he wanted to go back, but something in him was hooked. Was it the adrenaline rush that he felt? Was it the beauty of the gold? Was it exploring dark places?

His whits slowly came back to him as he reasoned about why he wanted to go back. Soon, he figured, whatever it was, it wasn't worth his heart. Tomorrow morning, he would wake up, cross the river, and then return to Settlersville, where he thought he should live. He didn't feel worthy enough to live on Mount Yah. Besides, the bear guarded all of that precious gold.

In the morning, after Clay awoke, he gathered all of his belongings. He noticed Joshua's large staghorn knife jabbed into the stump where the mountain man had sat the day before. He didn't know if Joshua had left it on purpose or by accident. Clay could tell that the man was really concerned about his being unarmed. Either way, he couldn't leave a knife this beautiful out there for anyone else to take. He wrapped his hand around it and pulled it from the stump. As he looked at the knife, he noticed that etched on the blade was the word *faith*.

When Clay packed up his mule, he made his way across the river and back toward Settlersville. While he was walking, he reached into his pocket and found one piece of solid gold. It must

have been left there from the previous trip into the cave. He stood there and stared at this gold, and his heart began to crave the cave again.

"What am I thinking?" Clay asked himself. "If I go back there, I could die! No gold in the world is worth my heart." But he couldn't shake it. It was as if his heart was connected to the gold that was in that cave. He began to wonder if there was a way he could go back and look from a distance, and if the bear wasn't in there, maybe he could go in and get a little more of the gold.

Are you kidding me? You barely escaped from the cave last time. How dumb are you to go back? Don't do it, Clay! Don't go back to the cave. It's not worth it.

I am shocked how invested I am in the story. It's not just that I'm bored with nothing else to do. I feel as if I'm reading this for a reason—like God led me here into this cave to read this.

It was as if Clay had no control over his body. The desire for the gold had taken him over, and there would be no stopping him. He had crossed the line of no return. He kept telling himself over and over, "I'm just going to look this time. I'm not going into the cave. I just need one more glimpse."

CHAPTER 6

THE OTHERS

Clay finally made it within fifty yards of the cave. The hike back seemed shorter this time as his mind kept picturing his future life made possible by the gold he imagined he'd get. He'd show the townspeople, bankers, Mason, Baldwin, Adam, and even Joshua what a man he was after he returned with the gold. He'd outsmart that bear and get the gold owed him. Then, he'd have his life of more—his own homestead with a wife, children, horses, cattle, and money!

Clay crouched behind some rocks and stared at the mouth of the cave for what seemed like forever. Everything within him said to go the other way, but he was so close! He might as well get a little closer to see if there was another way in other than the opening he had been accessing. As he came nearer to the base of the rock face, he was startled when he saw someone else climbing up toward the mouth of the cave. Quickly, Clay ducked down low to the ground so he wouldn't be seen.

To Clay's surprise, it was none other than the sheriff of Settlersville, Sheriff Henry. *How could this man, why would this man who was so respected in the community, be sneaking into the cave?*

When the sheriff got atop the ledge, he walked over toward the waterfall. Next, Clay saw the bear come out through the waterfall.

This must be another way into the cave! Clay surmised.

The sheriff hung his head and walked under the waterfall with the bear returning behind him.

Clay was intrigued. Actually, he was shocked to see the lawman there with the bear, so he waited a little while and then made his way up the rocky cliff, cautiously climbing in behind them.

Once Clay had moved further into the cave and away from the sound of the waterfall, he could not see the two who had entered the cave ahead of him, but he could hear their conversation echoing back toward him. He knew well enough to stay low and close to the cave's wall. Crouching down, he overheard the sheriff ask the bear, "How much longer do I have to come here?"

"Until your debt is paid," said the bear, "and besides, you love it here. You are the one who keeps coming back."

"Yeah, but when I came ten years ago, I didn't think I would be in this deep. I come every night when my family goes to sleep. I even lie to them and tell them I have to work late so I can sneak up here. I can't live like this anymore. It's killing me."

The sheriff and the bear began to walk through the bitter stream that was the source of the waterfall that initially drew Clay to the cave. In an instant, they were gone. It was as if they disappeared into the wall of the cave. *There must be an opening that either connects back to the cavern I've been mining in or maybe it goes somewhere else—where there's more gold?* Clay was intrigued. He had to find out where they went.

As Clay slowly waded into the water, he tried his hardest to locate the opening. Clay walked through the deluge of water and got on the other side of the stream. This revealed another tunnel where he could hear the clanging of pickaxes echoing through the tunnel and see a dim flicker of a torch at the other end. He began to walk carefully down the tunnel and deeper into the cave. That is when he saw it. The most visually gratifying room he had been in. Clay loved it. Clay never wanted to leave.

The walls were clusters of gold and silver. It seemed as if the walls of the cavern were made from these precious metals. Clay also noticed the beauty of diamonds and other precious stones in the walls. He was slowly coming out of his visual experience when a pounding sound started catching his attention. As he began to look around, he saw thousands of men and women in this cavern swinging pickaxes at the walls. He recognized a lot of them from town. The bank teller and manager were there. Then, there were some women and other townsfolk Clay remembered passing on his way through town the first day.

The pickaxes striking the walls wasn't all he heard. *Clang! Clang!* Clay looked at the people and saw that the clanging came from their chains. *They're slaves of the bear!* They didn't want to be there, but they didn't have a choice. He noticed that some had wounds on them from where they must have tried to fight the bear.

Taking his eyes off the chains of the townspeople, he began to fixate on the beauty of the cave once again. For a moment, he viewed the chains as a worthy trade for the beauty and riches of the cave. But as Clay looked on, his right eye began to feel strange. He put his hand up to his right eye to see if it had started bleeding. Taking his hand away from his face, he saw no blood on his hand. Touching his eye again, it felt as if the swelling had gone down. He closed his left eye and realized the swelling must have gone down because he was actually seeing out of his right eye.

That balm from Joshua must have done the trick!

Clay opened his left eye, and using both eyes, he looked at the wall across from him. Something weird happened. It was as if his brain was getting different signals. He covered the right eye and saw the glistening room of beauty and pleasure. It looked as it had when he first entered. Then, Clay closed his left eye, and what he saw shocked him. The walls were not gold and silver but the dirtiest coal he had ever seen. He continued covering one eye at a time and seeing the difference between the two sights, trying to understand what was going on. One eye saw gold and silver while the other eye only saw the blackest coal.

After a moment, it was as if the deception had been lifted off him, and Clay came to his senses. *How could I have been so deceived?* This was Clay's moment of awakening. He knew the truth, and it had set him free.

He turned around and began to run out of the cave, nevermore to return. He began to realize there wasn't an ounce of gold in the cave, only dirty black coal, good for nothing but burning.

Clay began to run. He ran faster and faster because he wasn't about to get enslaved to the bear in the cave. He ran straight toward what he thought was the light of day outside the cave, passing the opening he had entered only moments before. Just as he got to what he could then see was the mouth of the cave, an enormous figure stood in front of the light, almost completely blocking the opening. It was the bear!

Clay stopped in his tracks, staring eye to eye with the beast.

"Leaving already?" asked the bear as if he had no intention of letting Clay get out.

"Yes, I'm leaving, and I'm never coming back! My eyes have been opened to the truth. The gold, the silver, everything in here is fake!"

When Clay said that, the bear stood on his hind legs and belted out a terrifying howl that must have echoed all the way down to Settlersville. Clay's initial reaction was fear, but he couldn't back down this time. His freedom was on the line. Clay wasn't going to go down without a fight. He pushed passed his fear and ran as hard as he could at the bear.

Leaping onto the animal, Clay struck him with all his strength, punching and pounding away on the beast.

With one swipe of its paw, the bear hurled Clay through the air, causing him to crash into the cavern's wall. Clay slid down the wall to the ground, and then everything went dark as he lost consciousness.

As Clay slowly regained consciousness, he could taste blood in his mouth and could feel something tugging on his arm. It was the bear. Clay managed to see that the bear had his arm in its mouth. The warm breath and drool covered his arm. His head hurt, and he was so dazed he could hardly move. At first he was confused, but then he realized the bear was dragging him into the heart of the cave—to be its slave forever.

As he was being pulled away, and the light of the outside world grew dimmer and dimmer, Clay began to resign himself to his fate. No Mount Yah, no family, no purpose, only a life bound to slaving for something that was totally fake.

———

"I can't believe what I'm reading. I told Clay not to go back into the cave! But what did he do? He had to go back. He had to get the gold. The last time couldn't be the last time!"

As I vent about the story's awful turn, my own thoughts go back to my room at home when I was sitting on the bed disgusted by my having viewed pornography. I remember saying to myself, "This time it will be different. Now, *this* will be my *last* time!"

Suddenly, I stand up. My mind explodes at the realization that I'm Clay—that I'm no different than he was. "That bear for me is the bear of pornography. I've been a slave to something that's not even real. It's fake!" I holler out from the opening of the cave, my words flying into the outside world.

For so long I have been allured by the false beauty of pornography. I have been deceived into thinking I am in control of it, but in reality I have been its slave.

I have felt the same hopelessness as Clay. I have had two voices in my head fighting for control. I have tried to listen to the voice of warning—to do what's right. I have tried to overcome this more times than I can count. I have fought tooth and nail for freedom but always get dragged right back into the dark cavern.

This can't be it, God, the end of the story. My story can't be over!

I pick the book up, flipping to the next page to see if it's over for me and Clay.

—⇀

As he was being dragged farther away from the light, Clay saw the outline of a man step into the mouth of the cave.

"Bear!" shouted the man.

The bear spun around as if he knew who it was that called him.

"Loose him from his bonds, and let him go."

"No, he is mine! I have him, and I will have his heart!"

"You have deceived him into believing that the gold in this mountain is real, this whole cave is built upon lies, and you will not have him."

When the man said that, the bear shook its head, flinging Clay across the cave. Dropping the chain it had hanging from its paw, it stood on its hind legs and let out a horrific roar, again shaking the entire mountain.

The bear came down on all four legs and began to run toward the man with all of its strength. Clay couldn't believe his eyes as he witnessed the man charge fearlessly toward the beast with eyes of fire. The bear stood up on its two back legs right before colliding with the man. The two crashed with such force that the bear was knocked backward onto its back.

With the bear down, Clay could clearly identify the man. It was the mountain man, Joshua!

Now on top of the bear, Joshua rained down a fury of fists on its head, snout, and eyes. The two rolled out of the cave onto the ledge. Joshua had both of his hands pressing under the throat of the bear, holding its head and teeth away from his body. In the fight, the bear had momentarily bested Joshua, gaining the upper position.

Moving its mouth within inches of Joshua's neck, the bear was closing in for the kill. The bear sunk its claws slowly into Joshua's arms and began to pull at his flesh. Clay didn't know how Joshua was going to get out alive.

With a sudden motion, Joshua pulled out his tomahawk from his belt and struck the animal's right shoulder, stunning the bear and allowing Joshua to get out from under it. Jumping to its feet, the bear swung around and quickly knocked Joshua into the rock face alongside the cave, leaving him cornered and dazed. Joshua was covered in blood, Clay didn't know if it was his blood or the bear's, but whosever it was, Joshua was soaked in it.

The bear walked slowly toward Joshua. Joshua stood to his feet, his eyes flaming stronger than they appeared at the beginning. It made Clay think, *Joshua wants to save me more than the bear wants to enslave me.* Clay knew that Joshua was willing to die for him that day if it meant that, by doing so, he would get to go free.

The bear stood and towered over Joshua. It was about to deliver what Clay figured would be the final blow. In an instant, Clay remembered the knife that Joshua left for him the night of their first encounter around the fire. He reached to his belt and pulled it from its sheath. With the little strength he had left, Clay threw the knife, and it landed by Joshua's feet.

In one fast motion, Joshua picked it up and then plunged it deep into the heart of the bear. With the knife fully inserted, Joshua held onto the handle and drove the beast back until they both fell off the ledge.

Clay could hear the rocks crashing and trees cracking as the man and monster fell, finally meeting the ground with a loud *crash!* Clay pulled himself to the ledge and tried to slide down the rock face to see if Joshua was okay.

Clay had a rough tumble down to the base of the bluffs. He managed to stand and found Joshua stretched out on top of the bear with his hand still on the knife that stuck out of the beast's chest.

Clay reached his hand to feel for Joshua's pulse. When Clay touched him, Joshua rolled over off the bear. He was alive! Miraculously, though he was wounded in the fight, Joshua was unharmed by the fall.

Clay was more than grateful. He couldn't believe someone would risk his life for him, especially someone he originally refused to let help him.

The bear lay there. It was dead. Clay couldn't look at it for long because doing so brought back the painful memories of being trapped by the bear or possibly being enslaved by it forever.

Clay kept thinking, *What if Joshua hadn't come? What if he didn't save me? I would be a slave in the cave with the others.*

Oh, Jesus! I cry. I put the book down and get to my knees. My chest heaves from the sobs I can no longer contain. The love of Jesus fills my heart.

Just as You used parables, Jesus, to speak to Your disciples and the multitudes who gathered around You, You have used this story to show me Your heart for me. For so long, I have been trying to win a battle in my own strength—a battle that You already have won. I have not been able to lick my addiction, but I was never supposed to handle this all by myself. I am not the deliverer. You are. All I need to do is throw You my dagger of faith, and that thing that I have dreaded would always keep me enslaved, You have conquered for me. You are my Deliverer!

I begin to see Jesus in a new light. I no longer see Him as a weak, feeble hippie in sandals, who walks around and throws flowers. No, He's the Lord strong and mighty. He is a warrior hero who fights on my behalf. His anger is not focused toward me. He loves me even when I have rejected His help. His anger is fixed upon my captor.

Jesus, I am not the deliverer. You are. I put all of my faith in what You did for me on the cross. Lord of Hosts, break every chain off me.

The weight I carried, the weight that pressed sorely on my soul, lifts off me. The bonds that have held me captive break. I am free. I am released. I sit back down as I remember that Clay's story isn't over yet.

CHAPTER 7

RESTORED

Clay ripped the knife from the chest of the bear and began to make his way to climb the cliff. "We have to go back," he said to Joshua. "We have to go and set the others free."

"We will go back, but not now. Clay, we need to ascend the summit. We need to climb to the top of Mount Yah."

Mount Yah, Clay had almost all but forgotten it, and now he was free to go. The bear was dead, and he was indebted to it no more.

Joshua sat down next to the bear, "Clay, may I see the knife that killed the bear?"

"Sure," he handed Joshua the knife.

"Walk about two-hundred yards that way," Joshua pointed to the left, "and you will see my horse. Please go and get him and bring him back here."

Clay began to make his way toward Joshua's horse. He had never felt freedom like this before. Instead of constantly looking over his shoulder to see if the bear was going to be there, he had zero fear of it ever coming after him again. Nothing was there to enslave him anymore.

As he walked and got closer to where the horse was tied up, Clay noticed there was not one but two horses standing side by side.

"Virtue!" Clay exclaimed running toward the horses. When he got to them, he wrapped his arms around Virtue's neck. "I thought you were gone!"

Virtue looked healthy and still had most of Clay's belongings packed on its back, even his Hawken rifle. He could not believe it.

Clay untied both horses, took their leads in hand, and led them back to where Joshua was. As soon as he saw Joshua, he yelled out, "I thought I had lost Virtue forever. Where did you find him?"

"I found him grazing in a nearby pasture on my way to Mount Yah. It was as if he knew where you were headed and that you would be coming back soon, needing him to help you climb the mountain."

"I don't deserve a horse like Virtue, especially after I treated it the way I did and lost it."

"You might have lost Virtue before, but you will never lose it again. What is restored is always more precious."

"Joshua, how did you know to come and look for me?"

"I was close by to the cave when I heard the roar of the bear. I see so many people get enslaved there. They are either eaten by the bear or held captive there forever. I can't stand it. I want everyone in Settlersville to know the beauty of Mount Yah and freedom from the bear."

Clay then noticed that Joshua had begun removing the bear's hide. Clay figured that Joshua was going to take it back to Mount Yah and use it for clothing or a trophy. Clay still hated any sight of the animal.

Joshua finished up and loaded the pelt on the back of his horse. Clay and he saddled up and began the ascent to the top of Mount Yah.

"Stay close behind me, and don't get off the path. The way is narrow and rough, but I know it pretty well."

Clay obeyed, keeping right up with him the entire way.

Finally, they arrived at the summit. It was unlike anything he had ever seen before. Though they were on top of a mountain, there was green grass and rolling hills that spread as far as he could see. In the distance, he could see horses grazing, a river, and a vineyard. There were also homes scattered throughout the land. He could see children playing, riding horses bareback, and swimming in a creek. There were husbands plowing the fields and wives gathering eggs from the hen houses. The weather wasn't too hot or too cold, but just right. Everyone was happy.

As the men began to ride among the people, the people stopped what they were doing and came to them.

"Welcome to Mount Yah!" they exclaimed. "We are so glad you are here!"

"Thank you. Thank you." Clay's face began to cramp from smiling so much, and his hand was sore from shaking hands with different folk.

Joshua and Clay soon climbed down off their horses, and a man came over and took the horses' leads. He began to take the horses to the stables. "I'll tend to them. They must need some water and oats after the long journey," he said.

It was hard for Clay to let go of Virtue at first, but Joshua reassured him, "It's okay. On top of Mount Yah, Virtue can't be lost."

Clay thought it was time to set up camp, so he said to Joshua, "Let me grab my supplies so I can go ahead and find a place to rest."

"No need," said one of the townspeople, "Joshua has a place for you here."

Clay remembered Joshua's offer from around the fire the night he first met him. *Certainly, that offer doesn't still stand. Joshua practically gave his life to kill that bear, and now he is doing this? It can't be. It's too good to be true.*

Clay followed Joshua. They came to a log cabin. It sat away from some of the other houses. It had a beautiful view of the green landscape. It was farther down by the river. It looked like the home Clay had always dreamt of for himself.

Joshua walked up the front steps and unlocked the door. When Clay walked in, it took his breath away. It was everything he could have ever imagined and more. He walked around looking at every detail, and when he turned to look at Joshua, he was standing there with his arm stretched out, palm upward, and in the middle of his hand was a key.

"Thank you so much for allowing me to stay here until I build my own cabin. This is amazing."

"No need to build anything. It's yours."

Clay kept talking, "It should take me nine months to a year but—"

"No, Clay, you don't understand," Joshua said with a laugh. "This is yours! I am giving you the key to have. The house comes with a hundred acres of the finest land and includes fifty head of cattle and ten horses."

Clay was shocked. He stood there with his mouth hanging open for what seemed like forever.

"I don't know what to say," Clay fought to find the words. "Th-th-thank you. All I can say is thank you. This is more than I could ever have imagined."

Joshua just smiled. Then, he turned and walked out the door, hollering back at Clay, "Oh, yeah, dinner is at six tonight in your honor. We will meet in the center of the town around the fire. See you then."

Clay's eyes scanned across the room. He couldn't believe the furnishings, the fireplace, the kitchen area, and the bed. He walked over to it and sat down. Overwhelmed by the events of the day, he collapsed in a heap and drifted off to sleep.

A few hours later, Clay woke up. It was dark all around, and there was a musty smell. *Where am I?* wondered Clay as he sat up. He wasn't in his comfortable bed on Mount Yah anymore. The room he was in seemed familiar to him.

Stumbling through the darkness, his hands sometimes met the wall, and he kept lightly touching it to find his way. The walls were cold and damp. That is when it hit him. He was in a cave. "Joshua, Mount Yah, the cabin—it was all a dream!" he screamed.

Clay had to get out of there. He began to run as fast as he could when he ran into something, and he fell over. Getting back up on his feet, he saw what he had ran into. It was the bear!

"Going somewhere?" asked the bear.

"I'm leaving. I don't belong here! Get out of my way!" said Clay, panicking.

In his frantic urge to find a way around the bear, his eyes sought a clue for some means of escape. Looking back over his shoulder, he saw other figures emerge from the darkness of the cave. *Bears! There's more bears!* Clay couldn't tell how many, but knew he was surrounded. He was trapped.

One of the bears sank its claws into Clay's chest. He tried to get free from it but was powerless against the animal's hold.

"No!" Clay cried out as he sat up in his bed, drenched in sweat, with his chest heaving.

The sun was only barely peeking through the window, and there was a young lady standing inside the doorway.

"I'm sorry to startle you," she said. "I stood outside knocking when I heard you yelling. Joshua sent me to bring you to dinner."

"Oh, I'm sorry, I was having a——"

"Bad dream?"

"Yeah," Clay said, still trying to catch his breath.

"I'm Victoria. It's nice to meet you."

"I'm Clay. Nice to meet you, too. Give me a minute to get cleaned up a little, will ya?"

Victoria nodded, "Of course, I'll wait outside."

Clay got up and found a towel in the kitchen. There was a pitcher of water. He poured it into a large bowl. He took his hands and cupped them, lifting the water up to his face. He splashed his face and neck, then took the towel and dried them both, along with his hands. He pitched the towel toward the bowl. Turning, he tucked his shirt into his pants and walked out the door, "I'm ready now, Victoria. Sorry to keep you waiting."

"I don't mind. Now that you're ready, we can go."

Clay and Victoria arrived at the dinner. It was set up outside like a big picnic. There were people everywhere. Dogs eating under tables, children playing tag with no shoes on, and a large fire and lightning bugs lighting up the sky. As he walked to the light of the fire, everyone turned and began to clap.

The people pointed him to the table where there was a spread of food like he had never seen before. He sat down and ate so much he thought he was going to die. Then, he laughed so hard he thought he was going to puke. He had never been so happy. He had never met any of these people yet felt like they had known him his entire life.

Finally, Joshua stood up, and everyone cheered. He motioned with his arms for everyone to be quiet and said, "Tonight, we are here to celebrate a young man who recently made the journey from Settlersville to Mount Yah. Not only that, but he valiantly withstood the bear."

With that, everyone cheered, but Clay was hesitant. He remembered the battle and that he wasn't the one who defeated the bear. All he had done was throw Joshua his knife, faith. And the knife wasn't even his in the first place. It was Joshua's!

"No, Joshua, I did nothing at all to defeat the bear. I kept going back to the cave over and over again. If it weren't for you, I would still be chained there. All I did was throw you your knife, faith."

"That all is true, but without faith, I could have never defeated the bear. As for the victory over the bear, my victory is your victory."

The people rose to their feet and cheered so loudly that the entire mountaintop echoed with their praise! At that moment, Clay began to wonder if Joshua had delivered all the people around him.

They seemed to express a gratitude only found in those who have experienced a great deliverance.

Clay's hunch was right, for as the meal and celebration went on, he heard stories too numerous to recount of the rescue, deliverance, and escape from the bear. There were even some who bore the same claw mark scars over their eyes.

Near the end of the evening, Joshua motioned to Clay, "Come up here."

Clay stood up hesitantly and walked in front of the entire community.

"Clay, tonight marks the night where you go from living in the deep darkness of caves to living on the mountaintop, where you go from pursuing false gold and riches to living in real, genuine prosperity. The bear that once tormented you and deceived you has been vanquished now and forever."

When Joshua said that, two older men from the community came out from among the others there. They were holding something between them. They were carrying it on their outstretched arms. As the men drew nearer the light of the fire, Clay noticed something he thought he would never see again. It was the bear—its pelt. It had been made into a garment that the men draped around Clay. The head of the beast rested on top of Clay's, and the body of the bear hung down to his ankles, like something a king would wear. It made Clay look valiant like a mighty warrior.

The thing that once enslaved and shamed me is now a testimony to the victory I have. I will no longer be afraid to share my encounters with the bear, Clay realized.

Clay went on to live on Mount Yah for the rest of his life and even went with Joshua on a conquest to liberate others from the darkness of the cave. He wore the pelt of the bear every time that he rode into battle alongside Joshua. He told the story of faith's victory whenever someone asked about the scars on his face. He shared it with gratitude and honor.

I turn the page. The handwritten text doesn't start at the top of the page as every page before this one has. Instead, the text begins halfway down the page. I read it aloud:

"To whom it may concern,

If you are reading this, you found my story. Though you might not be able to believe every account of this book, just know that we all face a bear of some sort and we have all been deceived by the fool's gold that our hidden enemy has to offer. Heed my warning, though. Don't make the exchange. Don't exchange your eternal treasure for fool's gold. If you by chance find yourself in a battle with the bear, don't give up. Fight with everything you have and rely on the Dread Champion. He will always respond to your cries for help. You, my friend, have a choice. You can get up, brush yourself off, and fight this fight with faith, or you can be sucked back into the darkness of slavery. What will you choose? How will your story end? Will my story become your story, which is ultimately His story?"

Now, I know Clay's story is my story.

I once was so ashamed of my hidden secrets. Who I was behind closed doors was bound by the strong hand of the bear. Not anymore.

Just as Clay received the pelt of the bear, Jesus has crushed pornography and has not given me shame or guilt in return. He has given me a testimony. I am not ashamed of the scars from my past. They are all testimonies of how God has brought me through this.

Funny how the storm has finished as I have finished reading the last page of the journal. I gather my things and walk out of the cave. I can't get passed the symbolism of the moment. What once was a raging storm that surrounded me and kept me in the darkness of the cave is gone—and I'm free to show my face to the world.

I step out of the darkness of the cave into the warm, pure sunlight. I am stepping from darkness to light. I will no longer live in the darkness. From this day forward, I will live in the light as He is in the light.

THE EPILOGUE

"Come check out these magazines my dad has," my friend said to me. I was at his house when he said those fateful words, and I was about four years old at the time.

Oh, sorry, I probably should introduce myself first. My name is Jacob Peterson. And yes, in case you're wondering, the main character in the story you just read bears my name because, well, I kind of wanted him to tell my story. Though I didn't find an old satchel in a cave containing a story that led to a supernatural God encounter, I have walked in the same shoes as our main character. I have struggled with the bear.

The first time I was exposed to pornography was after I received my friend's invitation to see his dad's magazines. My friend walked another boy and me into his father's workshop, led us to a bottom shelf of his dad's workbench, and pulled back a curtain revealing a stack of *Playboy* magazines.

Looking at those magazines awakened in me a heightened sexual curiosity. It caused me to want to see more. Like trying to scratch an insufferable itch, I remember turning on the TV on different nights after my parents went to bed to try and find something inappropriate to watch. This was in the days before the Internet, so the primary way I would view pornography was sneaking a peek on TV or seeing the magazines when I went to a friend's house. I didn't fully understand what was going on and had no idea that I had an enemy who, with this, had initiated the battle for my life.

When I got saved at about the age of fifteen, I thought this hidden secret would go away overnight, but little did I know, the bear was only hibernating. In my church, porn wasn't really talked about, so I thought what I was doing was just a bad behavior that would somehow stop on its own. I wanted so desperately to be free but didn't know that path to freedom. I would have seasons of prolonged freedom only to find myself sliding right back into the pit of addiction.

Like an old nightmare, I still remember the feelings of shame, guilt, and hopelessness that I grappled with in my bondage to pornography. During this dark season of my life, I would consider giving up and giving in to my temptation. I would then throw a major pity party and cry out, "God! Why me?! Why do I have to struggle with this?!"

Then, I would hear the whisper of the Holy Spirit telling me, "When I bring you out of this, I am going to use you to bring a generation out of pornography." In those moments, God did what only He can do with a broken man: He imparted hope—hope that I would one day be free and hope that I would help others come to the same freedom. This book is the result. After I encountered the freedom Christ purchased for me on the cross, God used my testimony to bring breakthrough to those bound to pornography.

One day, I sat down in my office and decided it was time to begin my book. After all, "A journey of a thousand miles begins with a step." I opened up Microsoft Word and sat there looking at an empty document, watching the cursor blink over and over. Like a waterfall from heaven, however, the story soon began to take shape, and I found words forming in my mind, then coming through my fingertips, and finally appearing on the screen.

The first thing that came to me was the allegorical part of the story—Clay's written story in the journal. As I was working on getting that part of my writing completed, I knew I had to somehow relate my personal battle with porn. Pursuing how to do that brought me to the idea of creating a somewhat fictionalized story of my own life's narrative, and that's when I developed the story around which to deliver the allegory.

I thought of how Jesus taught through parables in the course of living His life. I believe it is a safer way to speak about my past addiction. Today, we are often encouraged to speak "our truth" and let everything else fall where it may, but there is such a thing as defiling others by providing the details of our past sins. I wanted to be able to convey a necessary message without causing you to become sullied. I think we both know what an addiction to pornography looks like in everyday life. What we need that isn't made as readily available for the those of us taken by porn are words of deliverance and healing.

To that end, I want to do what Jesus often did with His disciples: He explained to them certain components of His parable so as to convey to them its meaning. Those were the words that brought deliverance and healing to them. My prayer is that these will be words that do the same for you.

Clay

After I wrote the allegory, I still was undecided as to what to name its main character. At first, I chose a typical name, John, but that didn't really resonate with me. When I mentioned it to my wife, she instantly responded with, "Clay, because God made us from the dirt." *Boom!* That was it.

In Genesis 2:7, the Bible says that God formed man from the dust of the earth. This is such an amazing picture of the heart of God toward us. God saw beauty in what most of us try to wash off ourselves every day—dirt. He saw past the dirt and saw His children. Psalm 103:12–14 affirms this,

For as the heavens are high above the earth, so great is His mercy toward those who fear Him; as far as the east is from the west, so far has He removed our transgressions from us. As a father pities his children, so the Lord pities those who fear Him. For He knows our frame; He remembers that we are dust.

God knows who we are. He knows where we have come from—that we were made from the dust of the earth. Yet He pities us. He loves us. Think about that for a minute. God loves you and has mercy on you.

Your knowing these two things is vastly important at the beginning of your journey toward freedom. You need a revelation of the Father's love for you. You need to understand how He sees you, loves you, and wants to empower you to walk in freedom.

So often, we do not bring our issues to God simply because we are afraid He is going to smite us in His anger. Of course, our actions will have consequences, but our perception of God cannot be based on our natural thinking. Psalm 103 shows the heart of God toward us. He is able to have mercy and compassion on us because He remembers that we were formed from the dust—that we're clay—and from that place He has mercy on us!

Mount Yah

When writing this book, I made sure that I was writing to a specific group of people. I wanted my target audience to be Christians who love God, desire to do His will, and long to live holy. And yet, like I was, they are bound in a sin cycle to pornography.

Like Clay, you have decided to leave a life of normalcy for a life of pursuit. You want "the more" because deep down you know God has something more, something bigger, something greater than what you have experienced so far. This pursuit has taken you to the base of Mount Yah, otherwise known as Mount God. Psalm 24:3–6 in *The Message* says,

> Who can climb Mount God? Who can scale the holy north-face? Only the clean-handed, only the pure-hearted; men who won't cheat, women who won't seduce. God is at their side; with God's help they make it. This, Jacob, is what happens to God-seekers, God-questers.

In the New King James Version it says, "He that has clean hands and a pure heart" is the one who can ascend God's mountain.

If you are reading this book, it is because you have found yourself standing at the Mountain of God and haven't ascended because of the sin in your heart.

The Battle for the Secret Place

When we pull back the layers concerning this attack on your life, because that's what it is—an attack—it reveals a core motive in the enemy's desire to take you out through pornography: Satan wants to keep you away from the secret place.

Matthew 6:6 says, "'But you, when you pray, go into your room, and when you have shut your door, pray to your Father who is in the secret place; and your Father who sees in secret will reward you openly.'"

If you were to boil down the entire gospel of Jesus Christ, it would be this: God desired relationship with humanity, but sin separated us from His Holy Presence, so to make us holy, He had to send His one and only Son, Jesus, to the earth to pay the price for our sin. Plain and simple, Jesus died so that we can know Him. It is our highest honor and highest calling. Therefore, the enemy of our souls will do everything in his power to keep us from fulfilling this high calling.

Your sin cycle is about keeping you from God.

Your secret place was meant to be a place of joy and peace. It's not called *secret* because it's a place of shame. No, it's secret because it's the place where you are alone with God, where you meet with Him one on one, where you open yourself to Him, and where He reveals Himself and His heart to you.

We all know the feeling of going into our prayer time defeated. We repent for ten or fifteen minutes, then we hang our heads and leave even heavier than when we came in. Beloved, this isn't the will of God for your life! You were redeemed to encounter Him in your personal life.

Jesus died so that you can ascend Mount God. It's time that you put faith toward this fact: Since Jesus paid the highest price for you to know Him, He also made a way for that to happen. And a major part of that happens as you come daily to the secret place of prayer where you read His Word and practice His Presence.

The Bear

As with every story, there is an enemy. The enemy in this story isn't zombies, terrorists, or aliens from outer space. It is a bear.

I am sure at some point you wondered, *What does a bear have to do with porn?* Now, before you think that I have read *The Chronicles of Narnia* one too many times, I want you to hear me out.

Years ago, we had a guest minister at the Ramp in Hamilton, Alabama. He preached on the life of David. He referenced that, before David could take on Goliath, he had to kill the lion and the bear. He then drew a comparison that I had never seen before. He said bears represent sin cycles; like a bear that hibernates, they are here one season and gone the next.

This had to be one of the most frustrating elements of being bound by pornography. I would determine within myself to never view porn again, and I would hold up strong until I hit a weak moment. Like a rug being pulled out from under me, I'd fall and view porn again. It was a cycle. You're probably all too familiar with it yourself. You:

- View pornography.
- Repent.
- Try harder.
- Let your guard down.
- Fall.

Over and over again, this happens until you find the distance between falls are shorter and shorter. It's a miserable existence!

In the story, the bear lived in a cave that Clay was drawn into out of curiosity. So many times in my own life and in the lives of others, I have seen the trap that we walk into simply because we want to take a peek. Proverbs 27:20 says, "Hell and destruction are never full, so the eyes of man are never satisfied."

Clay slipped into the darkness of the cave because of his desire to see what was in there. In that place, he encountered the bear and the beauty of the gold, but he was quick to discover that the gold in the cave wasn't real. It was fool's gold.

Every person who has struggled with pornography probably remembers the time when they weren't able to "manage" their porn issue. It may have started off as something "innocent" and—as you've been told—"every guy does it," but it quickly turned dark when your entire world revolved around images on a screen. Soon, when it called your name, like a slave, you answered. I tried my best to illustrate this through Clay's having a close encounter with the bear in the cave, almost losing his life, which should have been enough to keep him away forever. Instead, the cave called him back, and he felt he had to answer that summons.

Rock Bottom

Do you remember when you realized you were a slave? When the issue became a problem and the struggle turned into slavery?

I do.

There is nothing more sobering than realizing you are a slave. That is when the light at the end of the tunnel begins to fade and the embers of hope begin to dwindle. This is when the questions begin to come:

- "Is there something wrong with me?"
- "Am I going to battle with this my entire life?"

And the biggest question:

- "Why can't I just stop doing this?"

If you are like me, you tried it all—all the altar calls, all the blogs, all the books. But the freedom never stuck. This is truly being rock bottom. Even though rock bottom is a terrible place to be, it actually is a precursor to Divine intervention because, when we still have strength to fight, we will always lose. When we surrender our strength for the strength of the Lord, that is when we position ourselves for breakthrough.

In 2 Chronicles 20, we find the story of Jehoshaphat. Jehoshaphat was surrounded by three vast armies that desired to destroy him and all of Israel. There is so much revelation in this story, but I want to highlight one simple passage. Jehoshaphat was praying and prayed something simple yet profound. In the midst of fear, discouragement, and hopelessness, he prayed, "Lord, I don't know what to do, but my eyes are on you" (v. 12). *Boom!* Mic drop.

There is such power and honesty in this statement. Jehoshaphat confessed he didn't know what to do. In an age of self-help and pride, we tend to always want to know exactly how to do something. But I believe when Jehoshaphat declared, "I don't know," it opened the door to the One who does know.

After that, he prayed, "but my eyes are on you." When you are at rock bottom, it is easy to become completely self-centered. Our prayers typically consist of, "God, I am sorry. God, I will not ever do that again. God, I . . .," and so on and so forth. All of our prayers and thoughts become centered on ourselves rather than on who God is. In this place, when our strength has failed and our works have collapsed, we are truly able to recognize the only answer for our sinful condition: Jesus.

When I had the encounter with Jesus that snapped the chains of pornography and lust off my life, I didn't have any other option. I remember praying, with tears streaming down my face, "Jesus, I have no plan B. You are my only option." In that place, true faith rose up in my heart and attached to the finished work of Christ.

The Dread Champion

In the story, Clay is in peril as he is being dragged to the depths of the cave, to a life of bondage and spiritual blindness. That is when our hero steps in, our Dread Champion.

As you have already guessed, Joshua the mountain man who rescues Clay is Jesus. I desired to depict Jesus in a certain light to drive the main message and point behind this book: Jesus is not who you think He is.

Living in a Western culture, we unfortunately have developed a view of Jesus that, to be honest, is just plain wrong. When someone mentions Jesus, our minds immediately imagine a white dude with shoulder-length hair, pearly white teeth that would put the people on toothpaste commercials to shame, all housed in a hundred-and-twenty-five-pound frame. He may or may not have a lamb over His shoulder. Why? We don't know, but it looks good.

Beloved, that is not who Christ is at all. He is a passionate, loving God, who is zealous for His children. The Bible refers to Him as a Dread Champion in Jeremiah 20:11,

"But the Lord is with me as a dread champion [one to be greatly feared]; therefore my persecutors will stumble and not overcome [me]. They will be completely shamed, for they have not acted wisely and have failed [in their schemes]; their eternal dishonor will never be forgotten." (AMP)

The term *dread champion* was used to describe a warrior who was so greatly feared that his reputation would spread around the enemy's camp, causing the opposition army to have dread. This is the Jesus whom we love and serve today, He has the name above every other name, and at His name every knee bows before Him! The very mention of His name causes the enemy to tremble! This is who He is, and you are the target of His passionate affection. He loves you enough to come, get you out of the cave, and take on the bear for you!

I had this revelation at one of the Summer Ramp conferences held in Hamilton, Alabama. One of the elements that marks the Ramp ministry is a deliverance anointing. The Ramp has so many stories of people, young and old, coming to an altar and being set free instantly. One of the areas that the Holy Spirit targets a lot in these conferences is freedom from pornography.

At one conference in particular, as we gave a very specific call to those bound by porn, I was walking through the altars, praying in the Spirit, and laying hands on those who responded. As I was praying, my heart began to connect with the heart of God for those who were there, crying out for freedom. Young men and women were laid out on the floor. Some in fetal positions, some prostrate, and others with hands lifted and tears running down their cheeks. Some were even crying so hard that their bodies were shaking. They were broken and desperate for freedom.

My eyes began to well up with tears, but not tears of sorrow, tears of righteous anger. In that place, the voice of God broke through in a way I had never heard before. He simply said, "Enough is enough." As my heart was connected with His, I began to feel the feelings Father God has for His children, and He was and is fed up. He is not fed up with you; He is fed up with the chains of pornography wreaking havoc in your life.

I am a father to two precious little girls. They are my world!! I would do anything for them. So, when I think about God as our Father, I can somewhat relate to the feelings He has. You see, if someone messed with my babies, I would choke slam them. Plain and simple. Man, woman, grandma, grandpa, I don't care. You don't mess with my children! How much more our Father in heaven, who gave His only Son for us so that we can be free from every sin that entangles us?

Visual Molestation

I would like to introduce you to a term that I believe perfectly summarizes what is going on in our generation. That term is *visual molestation*. There are two ways this term is applicable. The first is a little more obvious. Let me explain.

When a man or woman views pornography, he or she is visually molesting the individual portrayed in the pornography. The realization that you are harming someone else by your viewing their naked body or their sexual acts is quite convicting. We must understand that's serious business.

There is another application of visual molestation that I want to bring to your attention as well. Here's what we also need to understand.

When a young boy or girl is molested, he or she is taken advantage of sexually. I believe that we are currently seeing a new form of molestation in our generation and that is the molestation of the eyes.

In previous years, to gain access to pornography, you had to go out in public and purchase a magazine or video cassette. That within itself was just plain awkward! Imagine going into a gas station to buy a pornographic magazine and in walks your grandma! It carried a level of guilt with it that would deter many individuals. Pornography, then, was something that you had to seek after. Now, we live in an age where pornography seeks us—all of us!

With the rise of social media, brand marketing, and the Internet, pornography evolved with the times, and to increase profit margins, different entities began to market after a certain demographic. Like the crack dealer in a shady alley, these various entities pursue younger clients to generate lifelong clients.

The average age of a young boy's first exposure to porn is eight years old! Eight years old! And boys are not being exposed to a centerfold of a *Playboy* magazine; no, they're being exposed to hardcore pornography that they can immediately access on their smart devices. With the mere press of a thumb or swipe of a finger—*tada*—there is the image molesting the eyes of our nation's children, young people, and adults.

Before you think that I am just casting blame on the major porn companies of the world, I know there is a larger player behind this: Satan. Satan desires that boys and girls are exposed at a young age in order to tailspin them into years of sexual sin cycles. In order to keep them from burning for God in their youth, he has them entangled in a lifestyle of hidden sin.

This, my friend, is what has stirred the anger of the Lord. God is calling for a generation of young men to arise who burn for Jesus, not with lust! Now is the time for deliverance, and now is the time for freedom!

Jesus paid a heavy price for your freedom. Now is the time to walk in it.

You Are Free

When I came to the end of my journey, I was truly at rock bottom. As I looked at what the Word of God said, I knew that I wasn't walking in the fullness of what Jesus had purchased for me.

Jesus said, "Life more abundantly," yet my life was full of shame and sin (John 10:10).

Jesus said, "He who the Son sets free is free indeed," yet my chains taunted me on a daily basis (John 8:36).

The Holy Spirit through Paul said, "if any man be in Christ, he is a new creation, old things have passed away and behold all things have become new," but my old man was alive and kicking (2 Corinthians 5:17).

Why wasn't I seeing the fullness of what Christ purchased for me? I knew I was saved, I knew I loved Jesus and He loved me, but why wasn't my life reflecting it?

Finally, I came to Romans 6, a chapter that I have read more times than I know. Except this one time, I wasn't mindlessly skimming over it. I was desperate!

It's interesting how desperation activates our faith. When life is good, our faith is often dormant, but when a crisis hits, our faith is awakened. I needed God to change me. I had no plan B. I was like Clay the last time we saw him in the cave—right before Joshua came after the bear for him. I was being dragged away, my arm in the bear's mouth, headed deeper into its dark cave.

As I poured over the verses in Romans 6, I read that, through baptism, my sin nature died with Christ and that, when Jesus was raised from the dead, I was raised with Him! Verse six said that the old Jacob—the lustful, lying, shame-riddled Jacob—died, and the body of sin was done away with. It was gone!

Then, I read verse eleven, and my eyes were opened. It says, "Likewise, you also, reckon yourselves to be dead indeed to sin, but alive to God in Christ Jesus our Lord."

In that moment, I realized that I was waiting on God to deliver me when, in reality, Jesus had already set me free!

Friend, when Jesus died on the cross, we died with Him, and when He was raised, we were, too!

Our faith has to embrace this truth: Jesus has paid the price for our viewing pornography, and lust isn't something we have to live and struggle with it for the rest of our lives. It has been defeated on the cross. Our job is to reckon ourselves "dead indeed" to it. Then, we can live and walk in victory!

After the Word of the Lord was planted in my heart, I finished the deal by being re-baptized. As I was plunged underneath the water's surface, I knew the old me with all its lust for pornography was being put under, nevermore to return. When I came up out of the water, I physically felt myself being raised into newness of life. I had been baptized before, but this time it was different. This time I had faith for transformation.

Since that moment, I have lived at a level of freedom that I never knew before. Just as Paul wrote in Galatians 6:14, "May I never boast except in the cross of our Lord Jesus Christ, through which the world has been crucified to me and I to the world," pornography has been crucified to me and I to it. There is absolutely no desire to lust or to look at porn anymore. I have no filter on my phone. I don't live my life, looking back over my shoulder to see if the bear is coming back after me. I am truly free.

This book is simply my boasting in the cross. If it weren't for Jesus, I would be bound by this sin cycle, fighting to get free, but because of Jesus, I am truly set free.

Friend, this freedom is for you. It doesn't matter how long you have been bound by pornography, how deep you are in it, or how hopeless you think your condition is. Jesus' heart for you is steadfast and never changing. You might feel like giving up, but take heart! God has brought this book to you at the perfect moment.

Don't give up, just give in. Give in to faith, give yourself wholeheartedly to Jesus, and allow Him to supernaturally set you free. He is faithful and will not let you down. He is your "Dread Champion," who has gained victory for you.

Now What?

I have read many books that talk about this topic. They were full of practical and encouraging advice, but they left me thinking, "Praise God for you, but what do I do?"

In answer to my own question, here's what you do: You pray. Oh, I bet you didn't see that one coming. Don't skip this part thinking, "No, I've tried that before. I need something else. Give me something different!"

Hold on for a second. I want to address what will happen if you pray now. You just read a book with two things: my testimony and Scripture. Revelation 19:10 says, "The testimony of Jesus is the spirit of prophecy." That means, when you listen to what God has done in someone's life, it builds your faith to know that, if God did it for them, He wants to do it for you, and He can do it for you!

Secondly, you now have the Word of God pertaining to this specific situation in your spirit. The Bible says, "Faith comes by hearing and hearing the word of God" (Romans 10:17). This means the Word has given you faith for deliverance!

Put the book down, hit your knees, and close your eyes. Pray to your Father.

He hears you. He sees you. He desires your deliverance more than anything, so much so that He provided His own Son for your salvation.

I love what Romans 8:32 says, "He who did not spare His own Son, but delivered Him up for us all, how shall He not with Him also freely give us all things."

The Father has already provided the means for your deliverance. It's Jesus and all He secured for you through His death, burial, and resurrection. Simply access your deliverance and freedom through faith.

The second thing you need to do is come into the light. You see, the strategy of the enemy through the shame of pornography is to shut you up in darkness. John 3:19–21 details this for us so clearly, it says,

> And this is the condemnation, that the light has come into the world, and men loved darkness rather than light, because their deeds were evil. For everyone practicing evil hates the light and does not come to the light, lest his deeds should be exposed. But he who does the truth comes to the light, that his deeds may be clearly seen, that they have been done in God.

Did you catch that? Men love darkness rather than light because our deeds are evil, and those who practice evil hate the light.

First John 1:5 says, "And this is the message that we have heard from Him and declare to you: That God is light and that in Him there is no darkness at all."

When we make the decision to come into the light, we are putting to death the deeds of darkness and breaking the power of the enemy over us. In essence, we are saying, "I do not accept my sin, but I choose God instead."

I will tell you this: God put strategic people in my life to whom I could go and expose my sin. It was embarrassing, it was painful, but it was necessary and most definitely worth it.

First off, we must come clean to God in repentance. This has always thrown me into a theological loop. Why do I need to confess to God when He already knows I messed up? Hebrews 4:13 says, "Nothing in all creation is hidden from God's sight, everything is uncovered and exposed before the eyes of Him of whom we must give account." If He already knows, then why do I have to confess?

Confession demonstrates to God that I'm serious about change. It shows Him that I mean business and am willing to come clean to Him. And here's why—God cannot heal what I refuse to reveal.

After you come clean to God, you need to come clean to someone in your life. This can be harder than confessing to God because it reveals your struggles and your weaknesses.

First John 1:7 says it like this, "But if we walk in the light as He is in the light, we have fellowship with one another and the blood of Jesus, His Son cleanses us from all sin."

When you choose to bring your sin to your father or your youth pastor, for example, it now brings you into a place of accountability and puts someone in your corner who can fight this fight with you.

I don't know about you, but I love a good action movie from the 80s. You know, some good Schwarzenegger or Stallone. The storyline normally focuses on one person. Let's use Stallone, or should I say, Rambo, in this case. Typically, he has a problem, and in order to fix this problem he breaks out a machine gun and goes to war. Everything explodes, and he ends up killing three to five thousand men singlehandedly. This is very entertaining to watch but totally unrealistic.

If you look at real warfare, you will see that wars are not won by a single person but by a group of people who have one mind and one mission. They are focused, and they have each other's back.

Let me ask you, who has your back? Or are you a Rambo in this fight of purity, trying to gain the victory by yourself?

I want you to remember it like this: There are no Rambos in the fight for purity. Get a group of men around you who can challenge you to be the man of God you are destined to be.

Often times, when we think of accountability, we view it as damage control after we have fallen. However, accountability is actually designed for you to be held in check and provoked to deeper fellowship and communion with God and others. Accountability isn't meant to be an avenue for rebuke after you've blown it.

I have had the privilege of walking this journey with several young men, and I was always getting what I call *failure texts*. So, I had these men start texting me when they were being tempted. It didn't have to be a long text just an emoji even. I then would pray for the individual who sent the *temptation text* and followed up later that day to see how he was. This seemed to be very helpful to these young men. If you do something like this with someone you're walking in accountability with, it will lead to your not fighting your battle alone and help you grow in your freedom.

Reach out to someone, get real with him, and allow him to speak into your life.

Fair warning though, it isn't easy. It's awkward and often painful, but so worth it in the end.

Friend, don't quit. You may be reading this book and are at the end of your rope as you've tried to free yourself from the bear's grip. You've read the blogs, you've gone to the altar, and you've worn the purity rings, but all to no avail. I simply want to tell you not to give up. Keep pursuing Jesus and keep fighting!

There are two bells that I want to introduce you to. They sound the same, but they produce very different results.

The first bell is a bell that sits in the middle of a courtyard on a Navy base on the icy cold waters off the West Coast. There, Navy Seals do a grueling event called *Hell Week*. These men are physically pushed to the limit of human capability as they endure an entire week with little to no sleep and endure physical exercise the likes of which we will never understand.

Recruits have to get "wet and sandy," for one thing. They are required to dive into the cold waters of the Pacific Ocean, fully clothed, and then roll in the sand, allowing sand to fill every crack and crevice of their bodies.

During a five-and-a-half-day period, candidates sleep only about four total hours, run more than two hundred miles, and do physical training for up to twenty hours a day. Twenty hours! I once ran a 5k, and they almost had to revive me with a defibrillator when I crossed the line. Well, not really, but you get my point.

While the Navy Seal candidates are in the midst of this grueling training, there is a way out. All they have to do is ring a bell. That's it. Just ring the bell, and they can go back to their barracks, take a nice warm shower to wash off all the sand and dirt, eat a nice meal, and go to sleep.

All they have to do is quit.

All they have to do is give up their dream of being an elite warrior.

They are put through this because the Navy Seal instructors believe completing the training and overcoming the hardship is ten percent physical and ninety percent mental.

Listen, friend, your body might desire pornography and sexual satisfaction, but it is more mental than it is physical. If you can win the battle in your thoughts, you can win the battle over lust.

Whatever you do, never ring that bell.

When you are alone in your room, and no one is looking, don't ring it.

When your girlfriend breaks up with you, and you are feeling down, don't ring it.

When the bills are stacking high, and you and your wife get into an argument, don't ring that bell.

There is another bell I want to tell you about. This bell has made common men into champions. It has caused crowds to cheer.

It has also revealed the cowardice of many. It is the bell that sits beside the boxing ring.

When that bell rings, there is no backing out. There is no taking the easy way out. There is only one option: Fight.

Don't worry, though, in your case. This fight is not a fight between you and an opponent who is stronger than you. It is a fight against a defeated foe; for in your corner is the Victor, your Dread Champion!

The same Spirit that raised Jesus from the dead lives inside you; therefore, you are not fighting in your own strength, but the Spirit of Christ, Warrior Jesus, who lives inside you, is fighting on your behalf. And each blow you throw carries within itself the same power that conquered death.

Let this be your battle cry:

What then shall we say in response to these things? If God is for us [in our corner], who can be against us? He who did not spare his own Son, but gave him up for us all, how shall He not with Him also freely give us all things? Who shall bring a charge against God's elect? It is God who justifies. Who is he who condemns? It is Christ who died, and furthermore is also risen, who is even at the right hand of God, who also makes intercession for us. Who shall separate us from the love of Christ? Shall tribulation, or distress, or persecution, or famine, or nakedness, or peril, or sword? As it is written: "For

Your sake we are killed all day long; we are accounted as sheep for the slaughter." Yet in all these things we are more than conquerors through Him who loved us. For I am persuaded that neither death nor life, nor angels nor principalities nor powers, nor things present nor things to come, nor height nor depth, nor any other created thing, shall be able to separate us from the love of God which is in Jesus Christ our Lord. (Romans 8:31–39)

You are more than a conqueror. That is who you are in Christ!

So wrap your knuckles, crawl into the ring, and put your game face on. Like Clay throwing the knife of faith to Joshua, cast your faith in your Dread Champion and watch Him come through for you, defeating the bear, and granting you freedom to live life—and life in the more!

About the Author

Jacob Peterson is a husband, father, minister, and hunter. He wants to see people fall in love with Jesus, confident in their identity and passionate about their purpose. His message is for all ages - a simple challenge to live a life fully devoted to God in order to fulfill the great commission.

For several years, Jacob served at Brownsville Assembly of God as the Youth Pastor, Young Adult Pastor and Ministry School Director. He also served as a Location Pastor at Radiant Church in Tampa, FL.

Now, he lives in Alabama with his wife, Lexie and three girls, Rhys, Piper, and Olive. Jacob is on the leadership team at the Ramp with Karen Wheaton where he ministers during weekly services, conferences, travel events and in the Ramp School of Ministry.

For booking inquiries please visit:
www.jacobpetersonministries.com

Stay Connected:
Instagram: @jkpeterson3
Facebook: Jacob.peterson1332